A GREAT WEEKEND IN

VIENNA

A GREAT WEEKEND IN
VIENNA

Only eighty years ago Vienna was the capital of one of the most powerful states in Europe. It was a cosmopolitan city, at the very hub of European life, holding its own alongside London, Berlin, Paris or St Petersburg. Originally built as the head of an enormous empire, presiding over fifty million subjects and governing people speaking fourteen different languages, the Vienna of today finds itself the capital city of a much reduced alpine republic with a long and turbulent history. It has a considerable national heritage, the legacy of the Habsburgs, who reigned for six long centuries over this mythical country, in which it was said that the sun never set.

Vienna is a city of contradictions – the result of its eventful past and the source of its great charm. You may at first find it a rather colourless and staid city, restrained by its own prestigious heritage, but as soon as you begin to explore and uncover the true city that lies behind this initial impression, you'll discover the essence of the real Vienna. Sometimes described as provincial, conservative and static, it can also be a bold, rebellious, even iconoclastic place, sparkling and full of life. Artists and designers are busy inventing the Vienna of tomorrow in their hi-tech studios and lofts. Today, its image hovers between two opposites, that of the old and the new. This great contrast is demonstrated very clearly by two buildings, facing each other across the square, Stock-im-Eisen Platz, in the Graben district. On one side stands St Stephen's Cathedral, imposing and venerable, and on the other, the controversial and modern Haas-Haus. Vienna is the home of opera and operetta as well as being the cradle of psychoanalysis and intellectual discipline. The philosopher Wittgenstein was born in Vienna, as was Sigmund Freud. Yet the great psychoanalyst would have needed far more than a few sessions on the couch to get to the bottom of Vienna's psyche, and you may well find that you really need more than just a weekend to complete your own

examination of the city. So, just let your mood dictate which part of the city you explore first. Enjoy a stroll past tempting shop windows, full of delicious chocolate and cakes, stunning Art Nouveau objects, well-made leather shoes and green Loden capes. Make sure you cast the occasional gaze heaven-wards in order not to miss the ornate façades with their lovely architectural details. Peer into hidden courtyards and don't miss the buildings painted in 'Maria Theresa' (*Maria Theresia*) yellow with their contrasting green shutters. At dusk you'll sense the presence of the many figures

sensuous marble sculptures. The Ringstrasse, the great boulevard around the city, was built in 1857 to symbolise an era of wealth, industry and modernisation. However, the city's other 22 districts all have

charm. Vienna is elegant, sophisticated and peaceful, and jealously nurtures and guards its cultural heritage. It's interesting to think that, until 1983, audiences at Austria's national theatre, the Burgtheater, never applauded the actors at the end of a performance under the pretext that their esteemed emperor alone should be given an ovation. Having explored all these different aspects of the city, it's time for you to enjoy a different cultural ritual – coffee and cake in one of the remaining traditional coffee-houses (*Kaffeehäuser*).

from the past that haunt Vienna. Mozart composed *Figaro* here, and Beethoven's Ninth Symphony was performed at one of the palaces. Many talented and famous artists have passed through the city, including Klimt, Kokoschka, Schiel, Brahms, Mahler and Schönberg. Don't confine your wanderings to the Hofburg or the Schönbrunn castle with its mirrors and painted ceiling. Push open a few gates and discover beautiful churches with their trompe-l'oeil of angels and clouds, and delicate frescoes. Even the most ordinary-looking buildings hide magnificent stairways or

their own unique charm. They are easy to navigate, and you'll discover a very different side of Vienna, not often featured in the travel guides. There's the architecturally interesting swimming pool at the Amalienbad in Reumannplatz, with a wonderful Art Deco interior, or the Karl-Mark-Hof housing complex, the peach-coloured 'people's palace'. Stroll through the Belvedere gardens at dusk, when you will hear only the faint sounds of the fountains. Across the river are the post-modern skyscrapers, contrasting greatly with the fascinating old quarters of the city with their uniquely Central European

However, if you prefer the idea of a cosy tavern, try one of the Heurigen in the surrounding villages. A *Heuriger* is a tavern, usually in its own vineyard in the Vienna Woods (*Wienerwald*), where you can enjoy a glass of Chardonnay from the most recent harvest (*heurig* meaning 'this year's'), usually accompanied by a delicious selection of cheeses and roast meats. It was here in July 1895 that Freud had his revelation about the secret meaning of dreams as he gazed at the vast panorama of Bellevuehöhe. We have our own revelation in store for you – that of the true Vienna.

Getting there

CLIMATE

Situated in the centre of Europe, Vienna has a continental climate. Summers are hot and rather humid and winters are harsh and tend to linger with temperatures falling to as low as 20ºC/-4ºF.

WHEN TO GO

If you can possibly avoid the Austrian school holidays, you're well advised to do so. They take place from 3 July-4 September and at Easter (23 March-6 April or 15-25 April). Hordes of tourists flock to the Schönbrunn Castle and to Hofburg during these periods. Summer is not necessarily the best season for a visit to Vienna since some museums are closed and the opera takes a long summer break, as do the Spanish Riding School (*Spanische Reitschule*) and the Vienna Boys' Choir (*Wiener Sänger-knaben*). Try instead to visit during late spring and early autumn, when Vienna is delightful.

If you're happy to brave the cold, Vienna in the snow is a magical sight.

HOW TO GET THERE

Vienna is an ideal city for a long weekend; there's plenty to see and the town is easily manageable on foot. It's easy to get there from most capital cities in Europe and if you're going for a short break, the best way to go is by plane.

BY PLANE

Travelling to Vienna, you have a choice of airlines which fly direct from UK. Austrian Airlines, the national carrier, offers four direct flights daily from London Gatwick and, with Lauda Air, they share a service from Manchester every day except Sundays. British Airways flies out of both London Heathrow or London Gatwick with up to six flights a day. Buzz, one of the new low-cost airlines, offers three flights on weekdays, one on Saturdays and two on Sundays. Departures are from Stansted.

If you lose your ticket or need to reconfirm your flight in Vienna, you should contact your airline's local office. Buzz confirms bookings with a reference number so if you lose your ticket, simply go to Vienna airport, show your passport and give you reference number and you should have no problems.

Austrian Airlines
10 Wardour Street, W1
☎ 020 7434 7355 or
☎0845 6010948)

Booking your trip online from the UK

You can arrange your visit through the familiar high street travel operators or by getting online and visiting the host of dedicated sites offering cheap flights and accommodation. Decide what level of service you want – this ranges from simply booking the flight for you, to arranging hotels/guesthouses, car hire and other services. Your decision will depend on your budget and to what extent you want your holiday planned for you.

Thomas Cook
☎ 0870 752 0049
(Holidays)
☎ 0870 750 0316
(Flights)
www.thomascook.co.uk

Going Places
☎ 0161 908 7941
or ☎ 08701 616203
(for last minute deals)
www.goingplaces.co.uk

Campus Travel
(students)
Head Office:
105/106 St Aldates
Oxford
OX1 1DD
(Branches nationwide)
www.usitcampus.co.uk

STA travel
(students)
Priory House
6 Wrights Lane
London, W8 6TA
☎ 020 7361 6145
(Branches nationwide)
www.statravel.co.uk

British Airways
Waterside, PO Box 365
Harmondsworth, UB7 0GB
☎ 020 7595511
www.british-airways.com

Dedicated online sites
www.expedia.co.uk
www.Cheapflights.com
www.lastminute.com
www.bargainholidays.com

British Airways have a country-wide reservations number
☎ 0845 722 2111

Lauda
122 Collonnade Walk
123 Buckingham Palace Rd
London SW1
☎ 0845 60 10 934

Airlines in Vienna

Austrian Airlines
1, Kärntner Ring, 18
☎ 505 57 57 1789

British Airways
1, Kärntner Ring, 10
☎ 505 76 91

Lauda
1, Opernring, 6
☎ 7000-76730

Flight information in Vienna
☎ 7007 22 33

Getting there from outside the UK

Unfortunately, there are no direct flights from Ireland to Vienna. The quickest and cheapest way to travel is via London, where you can pick up a connecting flight. Ryanair, British Airways and Aer Lingus offer cheap return flights to London. From Northern Ireland, travel by

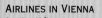

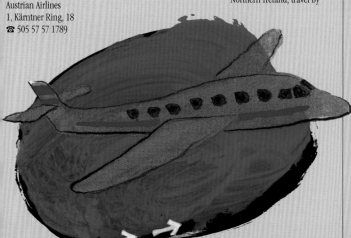

British Midland into Heathrow or by Jersey European into Stansted.

Lauda Air and Austrian Airlines both operate long-haul flights to Australia or New Zealand. Austrian Airlines also serves North America. Reciprocally, American Airlines, Delta and United all have flights into Vienna from JFK New York airport.

GETTING FROM THE AIRPORT TO THE CITY CENTRE

BY BUS
Vienna's international airport is called Schwechat and is 19km/12miles southeast of the city. Buses from the airport to the City Air Terminal bus station under the Hilton Hotel (adjacent to Wien-Mitte/U-Bahn Landstrasse) leave every 20 minutes from 5.30am to 11.30pm, and every 30 minutes from 11.30pm to 1am and 5.30 to 6.30am. The journey takes 20 minutes and you buy your ticket from the driver when you get on board. It costs ATS70 one way and ATS130 return. If you have a Vienna Card (see p. 36) ATS310 you get a reduction of ATS10. There are also buses every hour running to the Südbahnhof (a 20-minute journey) and Westbahnhof (a 35-minute journey).

For further information ☎ 5800 2300.

BY TRAIN
The high speed train (**Schnellbahn S7**) will take you from the airport to Wien Mitte/Landstrasse and is the cheapest alternative at ATS38 per ticket. However S-Bahn trains are less frequent than U-Bahn (metro) trains and are strictly timetabled. There are only two trains per hour (three during peak hours from Monday to Friday). The journey takes 35 minutes and trains run from 5.30am to 10.24pm. If you've purchased a *Netzkarte* travel pass (see p.36) then you'll have to pay a supplement of ATS17 for the extra distance to the airport, which is outside the city limits.

For further information ☎ 5800 35 398 or 5800 23 00.

BY TAXI
Travelling from the airport by taxi is the quickest and most expensive alternative to the bus or train. The taxi rank is outside the Arrivals Hall (☎ 7007 27 17) and will get you to the centre in 20 minutes at a cost of around ATS350. If you fancy a VIP arrival in Vienna, you can hire a minibus with air conditioning. Call the Jetbus Airport Shuttle on ☎ 7007 8778, 🅕 7007 8779.

BY HIRE CAR

If you intend to spend your time in the capital itself, hiring a car isn't really worthwhile and you risk doing battle with the one-way streets (*Einbahnstrassen*) and short-term parking zones (*Kurzparkzonen*). On the other hand, should you wish to drive up the Danube, explore the Wachau vineyards or tour the castles and monasteries outside the city, then it's worth hiring a car. You must present your driving licence and passport to hire a category A car for the weekend at ATS1400 (from noon Friday to 9am Monday, usually with unlimited mileage and collision damage waiver). You must wear a seat belt and children under 12 must travel in the back. The speed limit is 50km/30miles per hour in the city itself and 130km/80miles per hour on the motorway. Since November 1999, petrol stations sell unleaded petrol only. No leaded petrol is sold in Austria, but you can purchase additives for your own vehicle at petrol stations. *Eurosuper/95 oktan* costs ATS10.55-12.57 a litre/ATS2.30-2.75 a gallon, *Super* costs ATS10.34-12 a litre/ATS2.27-2.64 a gallon, and diesel costs ATS8.10-9.94 a litre/ATS1.78-2.18 a gallon. Prices fluctuate regularly. There are car hire companies at the airport, located at the west end of the arrivals hall which are open Mon.-Fri. 6am-10.30pm. You can also hire cars from offices in the city itself.

EMBASSIES

USA
9, Bolzmanngasse, 16
A-1090 Wien
☎ 313 39

Australia
4, Mattiellistrasse., 2-4
A-1040 Wien
☎ 512 85 80

UK
3, Jauresgasse, 12
A-1030 Wien
☎ 716 13

Ireland
Landstrasse Hauptstr., 2,
Hilton-Center
A-1030 Wien
☎ 715 42 46

Canada
1, Laurenzerberg, 2
A-1010 Wien
☎ 531 38 30 00

New Zealand Consulate
Springsiedelgasse, 28
A-1190 Wien
☎ 318 85 05
🖷 377 660

Avis
Opernring, 3-5
☎ 587 62 41
🖷 587 49 00
www.avis.com

Budget
Landstrasser Haupstrasse, 2
☎ 714 65 65
🖷 714 72 38
www.budget.co.uk

Europcar
Richard-Strauss Strasse, 12
☎ 616 00 16
🖷 616 00 16 30

Hertz
Kärntner Ring, 17
☎ 512 86 77
🖷 512 50 34

RED TAPE AND VISAS

Citizens of EU countries and other Western European countries require only a valid national identity card for entry into Austria. British citizens need to take their passports.

EU citizens can stay for as long as they like but should register with the local police if they intend to remain in the country permanently. Since visa requirements do change regularly, it's best to

check the latest regulations before you set off.

Citizens of the US, Australia, Canada and New Zealand require a passport, but no visa, and can stay up to three months.

CUSTOMS

As a signatory of the Schengen agreement, Austria does not make systematic customs checks at its border on nationals of EU countries. For information on duty free allowances for residents of US, Canada, Australia and New Zealand, see p. 83.

However, you should note that importing firearms, knives or ammunition is prohibited. If you want to bring your dog or cat into the country you must have a certificate showing vaccination against rabies signed by a vet within thirty days of crossing the border into Austria.

CURRENCY

The currency in Austria is the Austrian Schilling (Österreichische Schilling, abbreviated to öS within Austria, and ATS or AS in English). It's divided into one hundred Groschen and there are 2, 5, 10 and 50 Groschen coins, and öS20, 50, 100, 500, 1000 and 5000 notes. The Euro will replace the Schilling in 2002.

BUDGET

Accommodation will be your biggest expense (after travel), and coffee and cake at a traditional coffee-house can be costly. You'll have to add meals and a visit to a couple of museums, cafés and bars. Naturally it all depends on what sort of restaurants you go to and how many museums you visit. A rough guide to costs is as follows: ATS250 for a decent meal with a drink, ATS100 for entry to a

museum, ATS75 for a cocktail in a nightclub, ATS200-800 for a concert ticket and ATS150 for a three day travel pass. You could get away with spending ATS400 a day if you have a sandwich for lunch and go to a restaurant outside the *innere Stadt* (the 'innercity', ie within the Ringstrasse), where prices are generally higher.

HEALTH

You don't need any vaccinations for Austria, but you should take care when walking in some wooded areas, which are home to *Zecken*, a virulent tick whose bite can transmit encephalitis.

You may also have a problem with mosquitoes in the Lobau Park. If you're taking any medication, make sure that you have enough for your stay, since you may have difficulty replacing it.

If you have any problems, contact the Internationale Apotheke, Kärntner Ring, 11 ☎ 512 28 25, an English-speaking pharmacy. It's advisable to contact your travel insurance company before you leave and obtain an E11 form, which entitles members of the EU to claim reimbursement of medical costs incurred in Austria.

TRAVEL INSURANCE

Even if you are only going to Vienna for a weekend, travel insurance is still a good idea. If you have booked your holiday on a credit card, you

may already have some form of cover, and your possessions should be protected if you have a good home insurance policy. If you do need to buy insurance, the choice is very wide. Simply look in your

yellow pages, or alternatively, ask your travel agent to arrange it for you.

LOCAL TIME

Austria observes Central European Time, 1 hour ahead of GMT and 6-9 hours ahead of US and Canadian time zones. It's 12-13 hours behind New Zealand and 8-11 hours behind Australian time zones.

VOLTAGE

The voltage is 220V AC and two-pin plugs are used. Adaptors for three-pin plugs can be purchased before you travel or at the airport.

THE DELIGHTS OF VIENNESE PASTRIES

In Vienna eating a delicious and elaborate cake made up of several layers of cream and sponge is not just a pastime confined to elderly ladies in a cosy patisserie (*Kaffeekonditorei*). It's a Viennese tradition embraced enthusiastically by all, and often with a large helping of extra cream (*Schlagobers*). Pastry-making in Vienna is a highly respected skill. You can't go home without trying one of these almost Baroque delights.

INGREDIENTS AND INFLUENCES

Viennese pastry cooks still cling to the tradition of using rich ingredients, such as melted butter, chestnut purée, compote of prunes and poppy seeds, which are then combined in the most elaborate ways, often based on Hungarian or Czech recipes. *Palatschinken* is a perfect example of this. Succulent pancakes are filled with cream cheese, chocolate or crushed nuts, a recipe that dates back to the 1900s and an inventive chef called Karoly Gundel, who worked in Budapest. The dumplings, known as *Buchteln,* are Bohemian in origin, as are *Powidltascherl,*

pastries with plum jam and copious servings of apple. These filling desserts are particularly welcome with the onset of the harsh winter. No visit to Vienna would be complete without trying one of these local delicacies.

STRUDEL

Strudel is an Austrian pastry that's a source of both great pride and many calories, and you'll find it on all restaurant menus. Apple and raisins are wrapped in pastry (which should be as thin as cigarette

paper) and then sprinkled with icing sugar and cinnamon. Delicious when served warm, a *Strudel* can be filled with curd cheese (*Topfenstrudel*), plums or blueberries. Other specialities include Freud's favourite dish, *Guglhupf*, which at its most basic is a sponge cake baked in a fluted ring mould and sliced and the *Kaiserschmarrn*, a favourite of Emperor Franz Josef. This is a large sugared omelette with raisins and fruit compote, traditionally served with a fork.

SACHERTORTE

In 1832 Franz Sacher had to replace the ailing chef in charge of a banquet at the court of Prince Metternich. The young apprentice cook created a chocolate cake filled with apricot jam especially for the occasion, and he then coated it in even more chocolate. It was such a success that all the pastry cooks in Vienna immediately began to make the *Sachertorte*. However, for nearly a quarter of a century a battle raged between Sacher and his rival Demel over the exclusive rights to the recipe, whose secret (never revealed) lies in the quantities of the three types of chocolate used in the icing. In 1965, the courts finally found in favour of Sacher, and the firm continues to manufacture and distribute its legendary cake worldwide under the label *Original Sachertorte*. You can eat *Sachertorte* all over Vienna but it's only at Sacher that you'll find the extra ingredient under the icing – the apricot jam. The Hotel Sacher was built in

MAKE YOUR OWN *SACHERTORTE*

Ingredients for the cake: 150gm/5oz dark chocolate, 150gm/5oz soft butter, 6 eggs, 120gm/4oz flour, 100gm/3.5oz icing sugar, apricot jam. Melt the chocolate in a bain-marie, remove from heat and add the diced butter, sugar, egg yolks, flour and whipped egg whites. Cook in a moderate oven for 30 minutes, in a buttered and floured mould and allow to cool. Spread cake with warm jam.

To make the icing: melt 120gm/4oz of chocolate and 150gm/5oz of sugar in 1/8l/1/4pt of water over a gentle heat and stir until the mixture has a creamy texture. Use a metal spatula to coat the cake and serve cold.

TEATIME

Many Viennese will pop into a café or better still a coffee-house for a bite to eat. Some of these are veritable temples to the art of pastrymaking and offer an overwhelming choice of cakes, none more so than Gerstner, Kärntner Strasse, 11-15, where you can relax after a strenuous day's shopping. Anton Gerstner was 'court confectioner' from 1873 and made the desserts for the wedding of Empress Zita and Emperor Karl 1 in 1911. He continued to sell his *kandierte Veilchen* (violets in candy sugar) that the Empress loved so dearly. Another teatime treat is sampling a delicious *Sachertorte* at Sacher.

the 1870s on the site where Beethoven's Ninth Symphony premiered in 1824, in the old Kärntnertor Theatre.

VIENNA IN THE 1900S: THE SECESSION PERIOD

From 1896 to 1906, great winds of change and modernism swept through the Austrian capital. A small group of dissident artists, designers and architects were watching the new movements in art and powerful foreign influences very closely, and they decided to do battle with the stranglehold of conservatism in Vienna. This breakaway group of avant-garde thinkers was responsible for turning Vienna into an exciting forum for new, imaginative and experimental ideas and creative expression.

CHALLENGING THE ACADEMY

By the mid-19th century, rich merchants and industrialists had initiated the construction of the 'Ring', a horse-shoe shape of imperial boulevards round Vienna, that replaced the city bastions. It was lined with huge buildings, including the town hall, an important concert venue, theatre and opera houses and private palaces in architectural styles that combined Greek, Gothic and Renaissance influences. As a response to this pot-pourri of styles, devoid of any originality, nineteen artists

decided to 'secede' from the Künstlerhaus, Austria's leading mainstream artists' association, and to create a new aesthetic with its own credo: 'to each era its own artistic form, to art its own freedom.' The Secession movement was born.

GUSTAV KLIMT

The artist Gustav Klimt (1862-1918) was one of the first to react against the Ring and the official artists' association. He was the first president of the Secession and created a scandal with his Beethoven Frieze, a mural in three sections in which he painted nude women, floating maidens and emaciated silhouettes. This work can be seen

in the Secession building (see p. 57) and a leaflet explaining its symbolism is available. In 1903 Klimt turned towards more sensual imagery, with women painted on gold backgrounds reminiscent of Byzantine mosaics. His famous piece, *The Kiss*, can now be seen in the Belvedere.

OTTO WAGNER'S VILLA

Wagner's summer residence is a little way out but worth the journey. Restored by the artist Ernst Fuchs, current owner, the Palladian villa illustrates Otto Wagner's key artistic concepts. It's a grandiose building with symmetrical lines and stylised ornamental features with Jugendstil windows. Its apt inscription reads 'necessity is the only mistress of art.' The villa is located at Hüttelberg-strasse, 26, and can be reached by Bus 148. It's open Mon. to Fri. 10am to 4pm or by appointment, ☎ 914 75 86.

OTTO WAGNER

The architect Otto Wagner (1841-1918) was 50 and a key figure in the Viennese art world when he broke away from the artistic establishment. After the split he became an influential exponent of modern architecture, and, surrounded by brilliant collaborators such as Hoffmann, Plecnik and Olbrich, designed the Stadtbahn system including all the stations and bridges (see p. 58-9). Don't miss the two magnificent buildings on the Linke Wienzeile (see p. 57) and the Post Office Savings Bank (see p. 49). Wagner opted for pure forms, with a shift in later life towards minimalism.

HOFFMAN, MOSER AND THE WIENER WERKSTÄTTE

Josef Hoffman (1870-1955) was a pupil of Otto Wagner, and taught architecture and interior design at the School of Applied Arts. He was an important figure in the Secession movement and developed his own geometric style based on the recurring concept, or *leitmotif*, of the square, as his Purkersdorf sanitorium and Primavesi Villa (Gloriettegasse, 18) illustrate. The designer Kolo Moser took up this rectilinear theme in his illustrations for the review *Ver Sacrum* (Sacred Spring). It featured heavily in the many works produced by the *Wiener Werkstätte* (Vienna Workshop), founded in 1903 by Hoffmann and Moser with the help of the rich Jewish textile merchant Fritz Waerndorfer. The WW's work encompassed furniture, glassware, metalwork, porcelain and fashion, but only a few wealthy collectors enjoyed ownership of their pieces.

A GENERATION ON THE FRINGE

Around 1906 certain artists pulled away from the Secession and moved towards less ornamental disciplines. Oskar Kokoschka, aka 'O.K.' (1886-1980), was one such artist who made an explosive entrance onto the Viennese art scene with his expressionist-style portraits. Egon Schiele, regarded as Klimt's spiritual son and the last exponent of the Secession movement, died at the age of 28 of influenza, leaving behind works that dared to explore subjects still taboo in the Vienna of his day. Adolf Loos (1870-1933) had a brief relationship with the Secession, then turned against ornament and went on to design some of Europe's first modernist buildings, most notably the Loos Haus, on the corner of Kohlmarkt and Herrengasse (see p. 50). With its unadorned, austere appearance, it caused quite a sensation when it was first built.

VIENNESE DELICACIES

Ecology is an important buzzword in Austria, where the farmers are fiercely proud of their organic produce. In the markets you'll see more than 60 varieties of potatoes, and in one region alone, Waldviertel, there are 750 growers of poppies, cumin and culinary herbs. Fresh produce is the basis of the *Neue Wiener Küche* (Vienna's own *nouvelle cuisine*), and you'll find a wonderful choice of traditionally-made cheeses and cured hams.

GOURMETS AND EPICUREANS

In the 18th century, Vienna had a reputation for hedonism. Visitors felt that the inhabitants of Vienna had a much more sophisticated appreciation of the pleasures of life than those of other cities. Some even wrote that the Viennese behaved as if God had created them for the sole pleasure and purpose of eating and joked about how they would go for their Sunday walk, roast chicken in hand. It's true that the locals love their *Backhendl* (young chicken, breaded and deep-fried) but there's much more to Viennese cuisine than that.

COSMOPOLITAN INFLUENCES

Wiener Küche (Viennese cuisine) is very varied, the recipes and ingredients reflecting the multi-ethnic origins of the old empire. You'll come across Polish roast goose with red cabbage, Serbian bean soup, spicy meatballs from Slovenia, and Hungarian goulash with paprika, all on the same menu. These dishes are not known for their lightness, but in the last decade or so a new generation of chefs has made a conscious move away from the heavy sauces using flour and fat towards what has become the *Neue Wiener Küche*. Chefs are using fresh local produce (*aus heimischem Anbau*) and rediscovering natural flavours,

including celeriac, tarragon, juniper berries, wild mustard and rocket. This is the Viennese version of *nouvelle cuisine*.

TAFELSPITZ

The three main highlights of Austrian cooking are game (venison with wild mushrooms and Morello cherries), freshwater fish (either *Fogosch*, pike-perch from Neusiedl lake, or trout fished from the mountain streams as in imperial times) and finally, and probably most importantly, beef. This is the area in which *Wiener Küche* truly excels. In some restaurants you'll have a daily choice of beef dishes, accompanied by hearty *Knödel* (dumplings), breadcrumbs or pastry. *Tafelspitz* was the favourite dish of Emperor Franz Josef and consists of thick slices of boiled beef served with *G'roste* (grated fried potato, *Rösti*), a purée of horseradish and apple and a sauce with chives. You'll also find the most famous dish, *Wiener Schnitzel*, on every menu, traditionally deep-fried breaded veal, but sometimes made with chicken or pork. This is usually served with a potato salad in a sweet dill dressing (*Erdäpfelsalat*). Other popular dishes include *Zwiebelrostbraten* (beef-steak with crispy onions) and *Beuschel* (veal lung stew). A tasty soup (*Suppe*) is usually served before the main course and mainly at lunchtimes.

FAST FOOD VIENNA STYLE

If you fancy a sausage snack, then go to one of the stalls known as a *Würstelstand*. Try them boiled (*Burenwurst*), grilled (*Bratwurst*), long and lightly smoked (*Frankfurter*), spicy (*Klobassi*) or stuffed with cheese (*Käsekrainer*) These are traditionally served with chips, mustard (*Senf*) which can be hot (*scharf*) or sweet (*süss*), tomato sauce, gherkins, a roll and a paper serviette. The sausages aren't exactly delicacies but they're a good option on a cold day. The stalls stay open quite late, even after the theatre closes, and you'll find them on the corner of most streets. No visit to Vienna would be complete without a visit to one of these *Würstelstände*.

Remember to ask for some delicious bread (*Brötchen*) to accompany it.

BREAD ROLLS

The art of traditional bread-making continues to thrive in Austria, and in Vienna there's even a small museum dedicated to it, called the (*Alte Backstube*). It's claimed that you could eat a different type of Austrian bread every day of the year. In addition to the basic crusty white loaf (*Semmel*, or, if in quarters, *Kaisersemmel*), there's a huge variety of loaves and ingredients. You can choose from the long, salty stick (*Salzstangerl*), rolls with poppy seeds, cumin or sesame seeds, and big crusty farm-house loaves cooked in a wood-burning oven. There are more elaborate varieties, including *Erdäpfelbrot* made with crushed potatoes and raisins, *Kletzenbrot* containing rum, and *Birnenbrot*, flavoured with walnuts, hazelnuts and pears.

VIENNA AND THE ENVIRONMENT

The Viennese love nature and are very aware of their environment. There are 34,000 small gardens in Vienna in addition to large parks and substantial wooded areas. It's one of Europe's 'greener' cities, and there's plenty to do if you're a fan of outdoor activities. You can cycle on the old towpaths, stroll along the banks of the Danube or in the forest, and when the snow falls, try your hand at tobogganing in the Vienna Woods.

The Stadtpark contains many statues, the most famous being the Strauss Monument, which is dramatically floodlit at night. There are other parks worth visiting, namely the Augarten (see p. 66-7), the Prater (see p. 66-7), the Belvedere (see p. 58) and of course Schönbrunn (see p. 60-1), with its fountains, aviaries and rose garden. The Pötzleinsdorfer Schlosspark is less well known and is a paradise for children, because of its toboggans, swings and sandpits.

FROM ONE PARK TO THE NEXT

The Volksgarten, the Burggarten and the Stadtpark are all in the city centre and are havens of tranquillity for the locals, with their scented paths and floral displays. The Volksgarten is opposite the Parliament and was laid out as a formal French garden. The Burggarten is squeezed in between the Opera and the Hofburg and was landscaped in the informal English style.

THE ISLAND IN THE DANUBE

To control water levels and protect themselves from the devastating floods of the River Danube, the planners cut a parallel channel, the Neue Donau, and created an artificial island, known as the Donauinsel. This long strip of land, dubbed 'Spaghetti Island' by some, became a leisure park in the 1980s and various activities take place at different

spots. You can surf or take out a pedalo in the north, dive, swim or roller-skate in the centre, and enjoy a bike ride or barbecue at a designated spot in the south. Over 100,000 Viennese come here in the summer to swim and sunbathe in this rather regimented paradise, where nothing is left to chance. There are also bars, discos and food stalls, and in June the *Donauinselfest* takes place. This is an open-air rock festival with fireworks. In the winter you can enjoy a spot of cross-country skiing.

LOBAU

If the Donauinsel is too synthetic and arranged for your tastes, just take a 20-minute journey into the 22nd district. Here you'll find a network of woods, lush and humid meadows and cool ponds, all part of the national park known as Lobau. Nature is still quite wild and miraculously untouched here, though you can, admittedly, take a cycle ride round the

area, which is about 15km/9miles in total if you start from Bilberhaufenweg and should take about 90 minutes. You can take peaceful walks or swim in the river, a stone's throw from otters, turtles and 90 different breeds of bird, including the golden oriole and bunting. It's quite the opposite of the Donauinsel, with its fragile ecology and spontaneous,

nonconformist activities. It has been a naturist park for over a hundred years, and in this little patch of green you'll find an interesting mix of people all enjoying the fresh air and casual atmosphere.

THE WIENERWALD

When you've had enough of shopping and sightseeing, head for the Vienna Woods (*Wienerwald*), whose gentle slopes and wooded hills surround the 19th, 17th, 14th and 13th districts. It's time to take off your smart shoes, put on your Loden cape and head for the Hohenstrasse, which connects four magnificent panoramic viewpoints, the Hermannskogel (542m/1,778ft), Kahlenberg (484m/1,588ft), Cobenzl and Leopoldsberg. There are lots of walks to choose from, some more peaceful than others. It gets very busy at the weekends, but a good walk is the one that goes from Nußdorf to Kahlenberg and there are two or three bus

LAINZER TIERGARTEN

Hermesstrasse
Tram 62, Bus 60b
☎ 804 13 24
Open Wed.-Sun. 9am-4.30pm (April-Oct. only).

In 1882 the Emperor Franz Josef II built a new residence, known as the Hermesvilla, for his wife, who could no longer bear to be at the oppressive Hofburg. It was the surroundings that his wife enjoyed more than the mini-chateau and its decor, and today the imperial hunting reserve is enclosed within a 25km/15mile wall and is one of Vienna's wildest public parks. The villa is a stone's throw from the park, which boasts wild boar, wolves, deer and, in summer, the Lipizzaner horses from the Spanish Riding School, which come to exercise here. Enjoy the walks and the view from the lookout tower at Hubertuswarte (508m/1,667ft).

routes, should you get tired. Whatever you decide to do, the area is stunning and certainly worth a visit.

VIENNESE MASTER CRAFTSMEN

You only have to look in the shop windows in Vienna to see how important the glass and porcelain industry is to the locals. The art of porcelain manufacturing dates back to the Habsburg's encouragement of craft industries in the 18th century, and porcelain made in Vienna (*Wiener Manufaktur*) was second only to Meissen in Europe. Today the *porzellan* is made with Czech, Scandanavian and German components.

LOBMEYR AND BAKALOWITS

From the first half of the 19th century onwards, glassworks in Silesia and Bohemia provided the Viennese with their stemmed glasses (*Ranftgläser*) and stunning goblets (*Freundschaftsbecher*), while experimenting with new shapes, colour and composition. Towards the middle of the century, they had mastered wonderful new techniques, and the Viennese firm of J and L Lobmeyr very quickly became associated with three important Bohemian manufacturers. Together with the Riedel company, which specialised in blocks of coloured and compressed glass, and the firms of Lotz and Meyr, famous for the luminosity and perfect transparency of their product, they made beautifully crafted pieces heavily influenced by the Italian and German Renaissance styles. In 1899 the main competitor of the Lobmeyr company, Bakalowits, had the idea of approaching artists directly to come up with new designs. Amongst them were Josef Hoffmann and Koloman Moser, together with students of the School of Applied Arts in Vienna. Lobmeyr himself followed suit but several years later. This marked the beginning of the golden age of Viennese glass.

OPALINE

Hundreds of different designs were produced in Bohemia between 1910 and 1928, using sketches by Kolo Moser and Josef Hoffmann, who had a marked preference for translucent opaline with blue highlights embellished with gold. The works of both followed the principles of the Wiener Werkstätte (see p. 12-13) and were designed for wealthy patrons. They made vases with delicate black lines in the glass and jugs with wide stripes, whose elegance, originality and geometric designs made them stand out from other designs, thus appealing to those with more avant-garde tastes. Bakalowits, however, categorised his designs according to their prices, with different names for those destined for the general public, the middle classes and the upper echelons of society.

SWAROVSKI

During this period, Daniel Swarovski (1862-1956), who had established himself in the Tyrol in 1895, began to experiment with new crystal engraving techniques. In 1930 he patented the technique of embedding gems in textiles that would soon revolutionise the worlds of fashion, jewellery and accessories. In 1950, along with Christian Dior, Manfred Swarovski put the finishing touches to the creation of iridescent crystal. It became known as Aurora Borealis, or 'AB' to those in the know, and was an instant success with theatrical costume designers and dressmakers. Today the Swarovski firm continues to research new, exciting and original ways of implementing this method in the manufacture of stunning bags, candleholders and table linen, working closely with designers

such as Ettore Sottsass, Alessandro Mendini and Hervé Léger. Every year the Tyrolean workshops come up with stunning pendants that adorn Vivienne Westwood dresses,

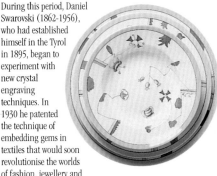

and crystals so pure and polished they're works of art in themselves.

AN IMPERIAL COMMISSION

Viennese porcelain, *Wiener Porzellan,* is heavier, thicker and slightly creamier than German porcelain and came onto the market at the beginning of the 18th century after master craftsmen were poached from Meissen. In 1744 the workshop was 'repurchased' by Maria Theresa and under 'imperial

WHERE TO SEE GLASS

If glass and porcelain are your passion, take a tour around the **Austrian Museum of Applied Art**, known as MAK (see p. 48), the informal museum of **J and L Lobmeyr** (see p. 102), **Wahliss** at Kärntnerstrasse, 17, **Bakalowits** at Spiegelgasse, 3 or at **Augarten** (see p. 12). The latter is seen as the official successor to the imperial and royal manufacturer.

and royal manufacture' very elegant pieces were produced. They were then painted with Austrian castles, still lifes and genre painting in the style of Watteau, by talented artists including Joseph Nigg and Franz Sartory. These included figurines, together with bowls, cups, plates and other vessels to contain the emperor's desserts. Viennese porcelain was at the height of its popularity, and there

were more than five hundred skilled craftsmen at work fulfilling orders from the court, Russia and Poland. However, fierce competition from Bohemia forced the closure of its doors in 1864, and it wasn't until the early 20th century that private enterprise purchased its stock and took up the torch once more.

CAFÉ SOCIETY

Cafés have long been a vital part of Viennese society – they have inspired generations of writers and played the roles of literary salon, games room and library. The café is an institution in central Europe, and in Vienna locals sit at marble tables and take time to reflect upon life and read the daily papers. Choose from one of the many varieties of coffee on the menu, sit back and enjoy watching the world go by.

A NEW DRINK

It all began in 1683, if we are to believe the tale, when royal troops from Poland succeeded in routing the Grand Vizier's army that had laid siege to Vienna for two months. As they fled, the Turks left behind 500 sacks of *chaoube*. The Viennese thought it was camel food and began to burn it. However, an Armenian traveller was lured by the smell from the fire and rescued the booty. Two years later Emperor Leopold allowed him to open a place to sell drinks not far from the cathedral. *Zur blauen Flasche* (The Blue Bottle) served a dark brew with milk and honey and coffee had been invented. A crescent-shaped biscuit is often served with coffee, as a tribute to the

Turks. The croissant came about at the same time, its shape mirroring the half crescent moon on the Turkish flags.

A WAY OF LIFE

Drinking coffee took off very quickly in Vienna and *Kaffeehäuser* sprouted all over the city. Under the reign of Franz Josef the *Kaffeehaus* became the place to go to hear the news. As Stefan Zweig wrote, the café was a sort of democratic club, accessible to all for the price of a drink, where you could stay for hours discussing, writing, playing cards, receiving and opening your mail, and leafing through a huge range of papers and reviews. Since Metternich had prohibited the

sale of newspapers, the Viennese adopted the habit of reading the press in cafés.

FAMOUS COFFEE DRINKERS

Cafés soon became the haunt of Austrian intellectuals, and Sperl and Landtmann (see p. 78) became the second homes of philosophers, writers and artists. For twelve years

QUICK GUIDE TO COFFEE TERMS

Brauner: small or large, black coffee with a small amount of milk

Einspänner: the traditional Viennese coffee, served in a glass and topped with whipped cream

Eiskaffee: iced coffee with vanilla ice cream and whipped cream

Franziskaner: large coffee with milk sprinkled with cocoa

Kapuziner: cappucino Viennese style

Maria-Theresia: mocha with orange liqueur

Mazagran: coffee served with an ice cube and laced with rum

Melange: small or large coffee with equal measures of frothed milk and coffee

Mit doppelschlag: coffee with a double helping of whipped cream

Original flaker: espresso with rum and cognac

Schwarzer: small black coffee

Verkehrt: coffee with more milk than coffee

Gustav Mahler

of its minimalist interior. Poems were written and pamphlets drawn up in many a *Kaffeehaus*, but for some like Altenberg, the café was simply a home away from home. After the fall of the monarchy, however, many cafés closed their doors.

THE NEW CAFES

The golden age of the café finally came to an end and small espresso bars took over in popularity. However, recent times have seen something of a café renaissance and the Café Central, once relegated to the archives, has been renovated, and talented architects such as Hermann Czech have restored its interior and made it into a meeting-place once more. It's housed in the Palais Ferstel and was restored in 1986. At the entrance there's a model of the poet Peter Altenberg, and Leon Trotsky spent many an hour playing chess here before the outbreak of World War I. Revolutionary thought and intellectual rebellion are unlikely to be fostered by cafés today, but they still offer an oasis of comfort and tranquillity in the city, a place where you can read your script or write your

the author Grillparzer spent his entire day at the same table in the Silbernes Kaffeehaus. Gustav Mahler preferred to reflect in the Imperial, Alban Berg, Klimt and Schiele found inspiration in the Museum, known by those who frequented it as the 'Café Nihilismus' because

diary, play billiards, enjoy an Apfelstrudel or a sausage, or make a choice from an almost bewildering list of coffees. If cafés have lost some of their former charm, there are still some more traditional places that are frequented and enjoyed regularly by those in the know, namely **Tricaffé** (Bognergasse/Am Hof), **Blaustern** (Döblinger Gürtel, 2) and **Heissenberger** (Landstrasser Hauptstrasse, 97-101).

VIENNA: CITY OF MUSIC-LOVERS

Vienna has an extremely impressive musical pedigree. Haydn, Mozart and Beethoven spent much of their time in the city, as did Schubert, who was a local. Brahms and Bruckner were in Vienna when the Strauss family's waltz fever broke out. Mahler, Schönberg, Webern and Berg took up the musical baton in the 20th century, confirming Vienna's musical tradition as second to none.

L. van Beethoven

THE HOLY TRINITY

There was a trio of composers at work between 1780 and 1790 in what became the musical capital of Europe – Vienna. Haydn, Mozart and Beethoven were known as the great trinity. Haydn came from Hungary, where he had worked as choirmaster in the service of the Esterházys. Mozart was born in Salzburg and was called to Vienna by the archbishop of Colloredo to start a new career. Beethoven had come to the city for a few months and ended up staying for the last 35 years of his life. All three men composed some of their most beautiful music in Vienna, revolutionised the concerto and left their considerable stamp on the symphony orchestra and string quartet. However, with the exception of a few patrons, the Viennese public failed to recognise their genius, preferring instead the Italian style of music to which they were more accustomed.

AN UNRECOGNISED GENIUS

The Viennese found the work of the 'divine Mozart' incomprehensible. Emperor Josef II allegedly pronounced after *Die Entführung aus dem Serail* (The Abduction from the Seraglio), Mozart's least-known operatic work, that there were too many notes. *Don Giovanni*, a great success in Prague, was a dismal failure when it was finally performed at the Burgtheater in 1788. *Le Nozze di Figaro* (The Marriage of Figaro) was premièred in 1786 but its subject matter was found to be too controversial for the aristocratic audience, dealing as it did with a lecherous count and a servant girl. The rest is history – Mozart died penniless at the age of 35 from rheumatic fever, and he was given a pauper's burial in an unmarked mass grave in St Marxer Friedhof (St Mark's Cemetery) in Leberstrasse, 6-8.

THE NINETEENTH CENTURY

Schubert was Viennese by birth and his was also a turbulent career. He died of syphilis at

the age of 31 and left behind him a prolific number of works, including nine symphonies, the eighth being unfinished, and 600 rather melancholic compositions. It's said that he slept in his glasses so that he could start work the moment he awoke. Other personalities at work during this period included Johann Strauss the Elder, who composed the

monumental and not a little intimidating, and it took time for the public to accept them. Arnold Schönberg (1874-1951) was an early father of the 'Second Viennese School', who pioneered the 12-tone system and introduced atonal music to the unsuspecting

Viennese public. His pupils included the Viennese Alban Berg (1885-1935), who gave us *Wozzeck* and *Lulu*, and Anton von Webern (1883-1945), both of whom were hugely influential in the world of contemporary music, despite the latter's comparatively small output. Together they made the 'Second Viennese School' internationally famous. In 1913 Schönberg conducted a concert at which two of Alban Berg's songs were premièred. The audience became so violent that an ambulance was called for.

F. Schubert

famous waltzes (see p. 28), the German Johannes Brahms (1833-1897), and, lastly, Anton Bruckner (1824-1896), an Austrian by birth who concentrated on church music. It was during this period that the Opera and Philharmonic began to take over the role, which until now had always been played by individual patrons.

MAHLER AND BERG

A new generation of musicians, born in the reign of Franz Josef, also helped establish Vienna's musical reputation. Gustav Mahler (1860-1911) was in charge of the Opera, while also finding the time to write ten symphonies and five song cycles. His symphonies were

MUSICAL STROLLS

Beethoven
Beethoven lived in the Heiligenstadt district in 1802 (Probusgasse, 6, ☎ 37 54 08), before moving to a small house set in a vineyard in 1803 (Doblinger Hauptstrasse, 92, ☎ 369 14 24), where he composed his Third Symphony. From 1804 he lived in a house in the 1st district, Pasqualatihaus (Molkerbastei, 8, see p. 46).

Haydn
There is a small Haydn museum at Haydngasse, 19 (☎ 596 13 07), where the composer came to live in 1796. It was here that he wrote his great oratorio, *Die Schöpfung* (The Creation), among other works.

Mozart
The Figarohaus is home to Vienna's Mozart Museum and is at Domgasse, 5 (☎ 513 62 94). It's the only place where Mozart lived in the city that has actually been preserved. He was here from 1784 to 1787 and composed *Le Nozze di Figaro* (The Marriage

of Figaro). You'll find facsimiles of his original scores.

Schubert
Schubert was born in 1797 in the house at 9, Nussdorferstrasse 54 (☎ 345 99 24), known as 'The Red Lobster.' He wrote his final compositions at his brother's house at Kettenbrückengasse, 6 (☎ 573 90 72), where he died in 1828.

Strauss
The 'Waltz King', Johann Strauss the Younger (1825-1899), wrote The Blue Danube at Praterstrasse, 54 (☎ 24 01 21). Here you can see furniture, musical instruments and other Strauss family memorabilia.

All the above museums are open Tue.-Sun. 9am-noon, 1-4.30pm.

BEERS AND WINES OF AUSTRIA

In 1784 Emperor Josef II had the great idea of allowing Austrian vineyards to sell their wine direct to the public in country taverns called *Heurigen*. The tradition has continued to this day, much to the enjoyment of the locals, who are able to taste wines from the current year's harvest when they go on their family outings in the Wienerwald. Enjoy a plate of cooked meats, cheese or salad with your glass of wine in a cosy atmosphere.

OTTAKRING AND OTHERS

Austrians drink an average of 123 litres/215 pints of beer a year and Vienna brews its own local beers, including Gold Fassl from the suburb of Ottakring and Gosser from Styria. The beers are light, with a wheat base, and most resemble Bavarian brews. You'll find the local labels in all the bars in the city, and beer is usually drunk by the half litre or *Krugerl*. Some bars in the centre of Vienna, such as the *Bierhof,* try to be more up-market in their selection of beers and sell rare or foreign bottles, as well as some very fine brandies with apricots (*Marille*), quince (*Quitte*), gentian (*Enzian*) or juniper berries (*Wacholder*).

LOCAL WINES

Austrians tend to drink more beer than wine, but wine has a special importance in the history and geography of Vienna, surrounded as it is by vineyards. The Viennese enjoy red wines from Burgenland, which are often of excellent quality, and the most sought-after wine from this region is the *Blaufränkischer*. Grown on the border with Hungary, near Lake Neusiedl, it's a relatively heavy wine that goes excellently with game dishes. However, red wine accounts for only 13% of the national wine output, the majority of wine produced in Austria being white. The *Grüner Veltliner* grape is the most popular, taking up over one third of the wine-growing soil in the country and producing a light and fruity wine, while the Müller-Thurgau, also popular, is sweet and very drinkable. *Muskat-Ottonel,* on the other hand, has a nutty flavour.

THE BEST VIENNESE WINES

There are few cities that could boast vineyards within minutes of their centre. The 19th and 20th districts of Vienna are still principally wine-growing areas, with 400 people working in the industry. On the right bank of the Danube, you'll find the older vineyards, including those belonging to the Mayer family, who have been producing wine in Grinzing and Heiligenstadt since 1683. The current owner, Franz Mayer, is famous for his Nussberger, the product of eight varieties. On the other hand, on the other side of the river, Fritz Wieninger concentrates on Viennese vines and has had great success with his Chardonnays and Cabernets. We must also mention Herbert Schilling in Strebersdorf and Leopold Breyer from Jedlersdorf, who've made a name for themselves producing excellent red wines.

HEURIGEN

restaurants. Wine can be tasted at three stages in the maturing process: *Most* is wine that has just been pressed, *Sturm*

The Viennese come to taste the latest wines at the *Heurigen,* particularly at the weekend during the summer months. These wine taverns also serve roast meats, cheeses and salads, but some of the *Heurigen* are proper

is the wine still undergoing fermentation, and *Heuriger* is the final product from the latest harvest. The atmosphere is usually cosy (*gemütlich*) and relaxed, and can sometimes become nostalgic and a little melancholy. You

KEY WORDS TO KNOW ABOUT A *HEURIGER*

Aufläufe: spaghetti or grated potatoes with meat, sausages and vegetables

ausg'steckt: open (as indicated by fir-twigs)

Blunz'n: pork sausage with seasoning

Buschenschank: bar or tavern (ie *Heuriger*)

Doppler: 2 litre bottle

Gemischter Satz: wine made from different vintages of wine from the same vineyard

Grammeln: small pieces of pork for a fondue

Liptauer: cheese spread with paprika

Schrammelmusik: traditional songs and music played in a Heuriger

Verschnitt: wine made from grapes from different

can sit for hours on a wooden bench listening to the violin or accordion. Each local will have his favourite *Heuriger.* There are several in the centre of the city itself, but those in Neustift am Walde, Perchtoldsdorf and Stammersdorf are the most authentic. You'll know when a *Heuriger* is open (*ausg'steckt*), a bunch of fir-twigs will be hanging outside the door.

BAROQUE VIENNA

At the end of Leopold I's reign, talented architects, sculptors and artists, mostly trained in Italy, were all fired by the same passion for Baroque style, and competed with each other to make Vienna into a second Rome. Between 1690 and 1740, a period of just fifty years, they achieved their dream, building majestic palaces and ornate churches, which celebrated both the triumph of Catholicism and the glory of Austrian architecture.

towns and 65 villages in Bohemia. The wealthy aristocrats now wanted to build their dream homes, the fear of attack having gone. They approached Italian masters such as Andrea Pozzo, who designed the Jesuitenkirche (see p. 48), and Domenico Martinelli, whose Liechtenstein Palace was a copy of the Chigi Palace in Rome.

VIENNESE PALACES

One of the era's most influential characters arrived on the scene in the form of architect Johann Bernhard Fischer von Erlach. He was responsible for the palace of Schönbrunn (see p. 60), the winter palace of Prince Eugène (Himmelpfortgasse, 8), the

ART FLOURISHES AFTER THE SIEGE

It all began with the end of the siege in 1683 and the crushing defeat that the imperial troops under Jan Sobieski inflicted on the Turks and the Grand Vizier Kara Mustafa. Then began the 'Golden Age' of Vienna, when it finally established itself as the Habsburgs' permanent Residenzstadt. Baroque art and architecture flourished in an improved economy, and damaged churches and palaces began to be rebuilt. Work commenced on Schönbrunn and Belvedere, two of Vienna's most popular tourist attractions today.

RICH AND POWERFUL PATRONS

The Viennese aristocracy had become very prestigious during the 17th century and amassed vast fortunes. The Lobkowicz family, for example, owned 2

Batthyány-Schönborn palace (Renngasse, 4) and the Trautson palace (Museumstrasse, 7), as well as the Bohemian Court Chancery (Judenplatz, 11). Johann Lucas von Hildebrandt built palaces for the aristocracy too, but his style was not as influenced by Roman Baroque as that of his rival. Inspired by Venetian villas, he built beautiful 'garden palaces' (*Gartenpaläste*) for the Starhemberg princes (Rainergasse, 11) and Prince Eugène of Savoy, by whom he was appointed official architect. Palais Schwarzenberg was built for Count Mansfield-Fondi in 1704 and subsequently purchased by the Schwarzenbergs (see p. 58).

BAROQUE VERSUS RENAISSANCE

In the 19th century describing a piece of art as 'baroque' was derogatory. It was used by admirers of Renaissance art such as John Ruskin to express disapproval of art considered over-decorated and exaggerated. Heinrich Wolfflin defined the difference between Renaissance and Baroque art in 5 points. The most notable of these were a) linear v painterly – Renaissance art is linear with incisive lines and contours whilst Baroque art tends towards merged images and blurred outlines, and b) plane versus recessional – or differing concepts of space. Baroque art has a great sense of depth and suggested illusions of distance, while Renaissance art portrays depth within a limited area.

ORNAMENTAL FLOURISHES

This generation of architects was prolific in its work – 400 palaces were built or given a Baroque makeover in the centre of the city or its surrounding areas. The style was very ornate, as demonstrated nowhere better than at the Oberes Belvedere, the finest palace complex in Vienna (see p. 58). It has an unusual roofline, resembling a succession of green tents (thought to echo the Turkish camps during the siege or represent mosques), with four columns decorated with military trophies, held up by muscular Atlantes.

It was built for masked balls, receptions and dramatic firework displays.

CHURCHES

Churches succumbed to the Baroque fever just like everything else – their towers assumed the form of bulbs, onions or pumpkins, and their pulpits became lavish gilded structures. Peterskirche (see p. 42) was to become a model for many churches in central Europe, and Karlskirche (see p. 58) was a blueprint of the imperial Baroque style. You'll find wonderful examples of trompe-l'oeil, round-faced cherubs and elaborate frescoes by some of the most talented Austrian artists, including Johann Michael Rottmayr, Daniel Gran (see the wonderful ceiling in the National Library on p. 51), Paul Troger and Franz Anton Maulbertsch.

THE BALL SEASON

Every year after the famous New Year's Eve concert, which invariably concludes with the Radetzky March or The Blue Danube, one fifth of the Viennese population (or so the statistics say) change into their dance outfits and head for the balls. This means that, until the end of February, 300,000 tireless citizens are transformed into Prince Charmings or Cinderellas and together return the city to its heyday.

THE WALTZ CAPITAL OF EUROPE

There are a number of reasons why waltz fever broke out in the Biedermeier period.
Until then dancing took place only in the country inns in the surrounding areas and people danced the *Ländler,* a sort of country minuet in triple time.

However, at the beginning of the 19th century, the Viennese discovered the delights of the parquet flooring, and hopping around on the ground came to an end. Gliding gracefully over a polished wooden floor to the music of Joseph Lanner or Johann Strauss and executing a much more elegant dance, the waltz, became the favourite pastime of many Austrians, although some foreign courts deemed it an indecent activity.

LET THEM EAT SACHERTORTE

The waltz is characterised by its careless, almost superficial, frivolity – a perfect symbol of the way the Habsburgs lived. The closer the monarchy came to its demise, the more

it indulged in masked balls, operettas and dances. Today the waltz retains the same superficial sensuality but has become almost a religion for many people. Couples rehearse constantly, refining their moves and adding more complicated ones, in the hope of being selected by one of the dance schools and having the honour of opening the ball.

THE EXCITEMENT OF THE BALL

There are more than 250 balls on Vienna's dance calendar. Each profession and community has its own, from waiters and psychotherapists to customs officers and farmers. The most prestigious event is the Philharmonic Orchestra's ball with eminent conductors at the helm. There's a very precise order of service to be followed, and the dress code is

and Tyrolans wearing their individual traditional costume and others in masks, until midnight. If a ball is masked, you'll see the word *Gschnas* at the end.

THE OPERA BALL

The ball to go to, which also happens to be the most expensive at ATS2700 a ticket,

very strict. You must wear formal attire: long dresses for women, and tails, bow ties and white gloves for men.

A RITUAL SET IN STONE

Tradition dictates that the evening commences between 9 and 10pm, and that, after the arrival of the debutantes, the orchestra strikes up first a polonaise, then a polka, followed by a waltz, a few minuets and quadrilles. Finally, the call comes: *alles Waltzer.* With these magical words, every couple takes to the floor and dances until 5am. Beyond this protocol, each ball has its own rules, with Czechs, Styrians

is the *Opernball,* held in Staatsoper. This ball marks the height of the social calendar and is a glamorous international meeting-place. Photographers await the arrival of heads of state, royalty, industrial tycoons and rising stars to capture them on film before they are served rivers of champagne by uniformed staff. However, the collection of lavish gowns and obvious opulence are not to everyone's taste and the European aristocracy tend to snub the event, preferring instead to grace the dance floor at the Schwarzenberg Palace. The opulence of the *Opernball* is considered an obscenity by some. Another extremely popular and famous ball is the *Kaiserball,* which is held in the Hofburg and was attended by the emperor himself in former times. The two balls compete for position at the top of the *Ballkalender.*

THE CHRISTMAS MARKETS

Christmas markets in Vienna aren't just about fir trees and carp, the traditional dish served on Christmas Eve. They're full of the scent of spices and roasting chestnuts, and Christmas lights reflect on the thick snow. There's the nasty Krampus (the Bogeyman) and nice Nikolo (Saint Nicholas), who brings children gifts in his bag. The Christmas markets are full of unusual treasures and festive spirit, and they're well worth a visit.

SOZIALAKTIONEN

December is the month for collections for charity and good deeds (*Sozialaktionen*), including the Christmas bazaar organised by Caritas since 1947, which takes place during the last days of November at Pramergasse, 9. There are also 'Advent markets' which many Viennese parishioners attend each year to help raise funds for the disabled and those in need. The markets have been here since the end of the 18th century and were originally patronised by the aristocracy and later by the middle classes, who bought their Christmas gifts at the various stalls. The custom is to have a

look round at lunchtime or at the end of the day. To keep warm in the late November and December temperatures, locals enjoy drinking a glass of mulled wine (*Glühwein*) or punch. However, be warned that you may find that the glass of punch you purchase contains more water than rum and orange juice.

CHRISTKINDLMARKT

The most important of all the markets, the *Christkindlmarkt* (literally translated as the 'Christ child market') has been held in front of the town hall (*Rathaus*) since 1975. It takes place from the middle of November until Christmas Eve, every day 9am–9pm. There are two distinct sides – the stalls and the park. The wooden stalls are arranged in lines in the central alleyways and offer a huge selection of gifts, including Christmas tree decorations, wreaths, candles, multi-coloured baubles, an enormous array of wooden toys, Advent calendars and Father Christmas figures ringing a bell to a tune by Mozart. You can also buy wonderful food and delicacies and taste jams, stewed fruits and cakes made from traditional recipes. Make sure you try one (or more) of the delicious Austrian specialities, in particular the *Marzipan, Lebkuchen, Spekulatius* and *Weihnachtsstollen*, all of which are delicious.

THE ADVENTZAUBER

In the surrounding park, known as Adventzauber, there are lots of attractions, not least an area for children inspired by various characters from fairy stories and fables, including Puss in Boots and Pinocchio. There's also a miniature Post Office that

sells special Christmas stamps and greetings cards. Inside the town hall itself, on the side of the *Volkshalle*, there are workshops making Christmas decorations and cakes, all for children, and choirs singing the most beautiful Christmas songs every Friday, Saturday and Sunday, 3.30-7.30pm. After such a delightful treat, all you need to do is go to a midnight mass at St Stephen's Cathedral, a more cosmopolitan venue than the *Votivkirche*. You'll be able to hear Silent Night (*Stille Nacht*) at both places, so the choice is yours.

THE OTHER CHRISTMAS MARKETS

The *Altwiener Christkindl-markt* is held in Freyung from the end of November to 23 December, open every day, 9.30am-7.30pm. It's a very lively institution, where the world of Austrian arts and crafts meets that of popular music. The Karlsplatz and Spittelberg markets are more recent additions to the market scene and sell oriental jewellery, aromatherapy oils and incense sticks. Try to get to the Heiligenkreuzerhof markets, held on Schönlaterngasse from the end of November until 20 December, Sat. 10am-7pm, Sun. 10am-6pm. The markets at Schönbrunn Castle (see p. 60) are worth a visit, and there's an exhibition of Christmas cribs held in the Berglzimmer, which is on the ground floor of the palace's east wing. It's open every day 2-7pm, from 21 Nov. until 27 Dec.

THE TRADITION OF THE ADVENT CROWN

This is a relatively recent tradition, which is Protestant in origin. In order to create more light in the church for the Christmas Eve service, a Hamburg clergyman used to light a candle on each day of December on a huge crown decorated with fir tree branches. As the tradition continued, the crowns gradually became smaller, and the 24 candles were replaced by just four, representing the four Sundays in Advent. Their popularity reached the Catholic regions also, and nowadays in Vienna the custom is to have three violet candles and one pink one, which are blessed in church and then hung from the ceiling at home.

THE BIEDERMEIER PERIOD

In 1815, following the Napoleonic wars, the Austrian Emperor Franz I invited Tsar Alexander I, Friedrich Wilhelm III of Prussia and Prince Tallyerand to Vienna to try to find a peaceful solution to the balance of power. The Congress of Vienna cost the city 22 million florins and was a great social occasion if nothing else, full of balls and banquets. It marked the beginning of one of Vienna's most important cultural periods known as the Biedermeier era (1815-1848).

THE METTERNICH SYSTEM

The government of the day wanted to prevent those provinces whose culture and language were different, from separating from the State. These were principally the Czechs, Hungarians and Slavs in the South. In order to

thwart rebellion and impose stability, Metternich put in place a system of censorship that included books and newspapers, together with the opening of private correspondence and a network of secret police. Some of these

Prince Metternich

were disguised as servants in order to infiltrate influential families and embassies.

In 1848, after 30 years of repression and denunciation, the Viennese marched in the streets, demanding the return of freedom of the press. The government opened fire on the crowd and the resulting bloodshed finally forced the emperor to take the decision to force Metternich to resign and flee the capital. It's said he made his escape disguised as a washer woman.

WITHDRAWING INTO THEIR BIEDERMEIER SHELLS

The political climate in Vienna during this period had greatly

affected the mentality and behaviour of its citizens. Resigned and repressed, they had turned in on themselves, living very private, family-oriented lives. They would enjoy the occasional visit to the Prater or to a ball for a waltz or two, sometimes even a visit to the countryside, but they always had to be careful of the ubiquitous informants. Spies could be hidden in even the most remote and rustic taverns. Freedom was really only to be had within one's

QUICK GUIDE TO THE BIEDERMEIER ERA

At the **MAK** (see p. 48) you'll find wonderful furniture and other objects from 1815-1848. At the **Kaiserliches Hofmobiliendepot** (see p. 54) there are reconstructions of interiors from the Biedermeier period and a huge selection of chairs, and at the **Geymüller Schlössl** at Khevenhüller-strasse, 2, there are seven rooms decorated in Biedermeier style. ☎ 47 93 139. Open every day Mar.-Nov., Thu.-Sun. 10am-5pm.

own four walls, and so the Viennese focussed on their home lives and comforts. Their apartments were small and often cramped, forcing their furniture to be correspondingly compact. It was arranged carefully around their new domestic activities, such as sewing, reading, drawing and violin playing, creating *Wohninsel* (islands of activity) at the heart of their living rooms. They filled their glass-fronted corner cabinets with trinkets, stemmed glasses, cups for their regular hot chocolate and other products of the empire. The word Bieder itself

means 'upright' and the era came to symbolise a safe and bourgeois lifestyle.

FURNITURE AND DECOR

Cabinetmakers made chairs and chests of drawers from fruit trees, inlaid with wood from the lemon or sycamore tree. Carpet makers favoured materials with floral patterns or decorative features, in blue, pink, silver or fawn tones, following the fashions slavishly. At the end of the 1820s the bolder citizens opted for the 'giraffe' fashion, the first giraffe having just arrived

at the Vienna zoo. Everyone wore giraffe motif dresses, gloves and necklaces, and you could even buy a snuffbox with a giraffe on it. At the beginning of the 1830s, Chinese motifs and style usurped the scene and mandarins and pagodas became the order of the day for the fashion-conscious Viennese.

THE SMALLER PICTURE

The 'Metternich system' also exerted a powerful influence on art, and artists avoided the larger subjects of religion and mythology, renouncing the dramatic and monumental to concentrate instead upon smaller landscape scenes. Josef Danhauser, Peter Fendi, Franz Steinfeld and Ferdinand Georg Waldmüller painted 'Biedermeier' works in their early days, leaving behind pictures of flowers, evocative and peaceful landscapes and portraits of children. Their portrayals of the Austrian natural world were stunning, although its more brutal or savage aspects were always softened by the artists in the true Biedermeier spirit.

THE WHO'S WHO OF HABSBURGS

The Habsburg motto was *Austriae Est Imperare Orbi Universo,* or AEIOU, which translates as 'It belongs to Austria to command the whole universe.' The Habsburg dynasty ruled over Austria for more than six hundred years, from 1278 until 1918, exerting its powerful influence over Central Europe. Today its fortunes and fate are remembered in films and commemorative exhibitions, and the Habsburg influence is still hard to avoid.

EMPRESS MARIA THERESA

Maria Theresa is one of the great figures of Austrian history and the first Empress to ascend its throne. She reigned for forty years (1740-1780) as a dedicated reformer, establishing a modern, centralised and unified State. This was no easy task given the cultural, religious and ethnic diversity of Central Europe. She began by founding a military academy and a prestigious school, the Theresianum on Favoritenstrasse, where future civil servants were educated and trained. She transformed the faculty of medicine, abolished torture, reinstated the privileges of the Hungarian aristocracy, supported manufacturing industry and found time to have sixteen children, among them Josef II and Marie Antoinette, future wife of Louis XVI.

JOSEF II

During his reign (1780-1790) Josef II embraced the reforms that his mother had put in place with her sense of justice and clemency, but his enforcement was far more rigorous and radical. He abolished serfdom, founded the general hospital, opened the royal gardens of the Prater to the public and introduced compulsory education, even for young girls. His most famous reform was the 1781 *Toleranzpatent,* which allowed freedom of worship for non-Catholics and also suspended some of the restrictions upon Jews. The aim of his political strategy, which paid little heed to individual nationalities, was to level out society and centralise power, and his short reign has been described as having a steamroller effect

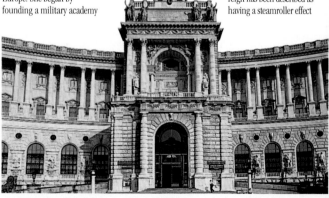

THE IMPERIAL ROOMS

Kaiserappartements
Innere Burghof
☎ 533 75 70
Open every day 9am-4.30pm
Entry charge.

The rooms of MariaTheresa and Josef II within the Hofburg have now become the office of the President of the Republic. However, those belonging to Franz Josef and Sissi are open to the public. A total of twenty rooms can be visited, all with creamy-white walls and gilded ceilings. Of most interest are the portraits of the young Empress Elisabeth, who spent a great deal time exercising to keep her extremely slim figure, much to the displeasure and disapproval of her mother-in-law.

on Austria. He decreed that German should be the language of bureaucracy, thereby causing much

bitterness in the hearts of the Hungarian intelligentsia and aristocracy.

SISSI

The Empress Elisabeth, nicknamed Sissi, was not a Habsburg but a member of the Wittelsbach family of Bavaria. She became part of the Habsburg dynasty in 1854, when she married the Emperor Franz Josef ('Franzi'), the son of her aunt, at the age of only sixteen. The whole of Europe knew of the beauty of this lively young girl with the peaches and cream complexion, who was too carefree and spontaneous for the formal

world of the court in Vienna. She felt unbearably restricted by court etiquette, and her pro-Hungarian sentiments were much resented. She did battle with her mother-in-law on many occasions, the Archduchess Sophie having removed Sissi's children from her care at birth to take charge of their upbringing herself. A succession of tragedies in Sissi's life, including the death of her young daughter, the death by drowning of her cousin Ludwig II of Bavaria, and the suicide of her only son Rudolf at his

hunting lodge in Mayerling in 1889 led to her becoming a solitary traveller around Europe. Using the pseudonym of Countess Hohenembs, she travelled between Budapest, Corfu and Madeira until being assassinated on Lake Geneva by an Italian anarchist in 1898.

ZITA

Zita became the last Empress of Austria. In 1911 she had married the great-nephew of Franz Josef, the young Karl. On the death in 1914 of Archduke Franz Ferdinand, who was assassinated in Sarajevo by Bosnian Serbs, and of Franz Josef in 1916, it fell to Karl to assume the difficult task of governing the embattled empire. His reign lasted just two years. Best-known for his failed attempt at negotiating a separate peace for his empire with the western allies, he finally went into exile in Switzerland in 1919. He died in Madeira in 1922, and Zita continued to bring up their children alone. At the age of 90, after 63 years of exile, she was allowed finally to set foot once more in Vienna.

Practicalities

HOW TO GET AROUND

BY METRO, TRAM AND BUS

The public transport system in Vienna is one of the world's most efficient. To get around you can choose the bus, train (*Schnellbahn*), tram or metro (*U-Bahn*), which operate 5am–midnight. The *city-bus* runs in the 1st district during shop opening hours and night buses run every thirty minutes Friday and Saturday, 12.30am–4am, starting from Schwedenplatz. A single journey ticket (*Fahrschein*) costs ATS19 and is valid for all forms of public transport. If you're planning on making more than two journeys a day, it's worth investing in a travel pass (*Netzkarte*) with which you can travel on all trams, buses, U- and S-Bahn trains within the city limits. A 24-hour ticket costs ATS60 and a 72-hour ticket will set you back ATS150. It's also worth considering the purchase of a Vienna Card (see p. 37). You must punch your *Netzkarte* pass at the beginning of your first journey only. Children

under 6 travel free of charge and under 15s can travel free on Sundays, public holidays and school holidays. Tickets can be bought at machines, ticket booths and Wiener Linien offices at U-Bahn stations. The latter are open Mon.-Fri. 6.30am-6.30pm. For more information, ☎ 7909 105. You can also buy tickets at newsagents and tobacconists.

BY TAXI

The Viennese don't normally flag cabs down in the street but prefer to queue at the designated taxi ranks. Alternatively, you can telephone for a taxi on ☎ 313 00, 401 00 or 601 60 (the extra cost for this is usually ATS16). Taxis are often black Mercedes and all have meters. A short trip around the city shouldn't cost more than ATS100 but the price is much higher at night

(11pm-6am), on Sunday and on public holidays. A small extra charge is normal for a journey from the airport to the centre.

By Fiaker

A ride in an open carriage, or Fiaker, is more picturesque and more expensive. The ranks are at Stephansplatz, Heldenplatz, Michaelerplatz and Albertinaplatz. The price depends on the duration and distance (usually ATS400 for 20 minutes or ATS1000 for an hour), but it's best to settle the fare before you set off.

By Bike

There's a good network of cycle paths in Vienna – over 500 km/310 miles, and nearly the same amount again is planned for implementation in the next 12 years. You can hire a standard bicycle (*Fahrrad*) at the train stations (*Rent a bike am Bahnhof*), especially Westbahnhof, Sudbahnhof, Wien-Nord and Floridsdorf. It costs around ATS150 a day and you can take your bike on the U-and S-Bahn Monday to Friday 9am-3pm and after 6.30pm, Saturday from 9am

and throughout the day on Sunday, at the cost of a half-price ticket for your bike. You can arrange for your bike to be delivered to your hotel by booking it by fax through some companies, for example Pedal Power. It will cost around ATS230-280 for four hours.

Bicycle hire companies include:

Pedal Power
2, Ausstellungstrasse, 3
☎ 729 72 34
Open from March.

The 'Vienna Card'

Die Wienkarte allows you to travel on all forms of public trasnport, gives you discounts at various museums (55% at the Albertina and 40% at the Academy of Fine Arts) and also in some shops, restaurants and sights. It costs ATS120, is valid for 72 hours and can be purchased from tourist information offices, hotels and at the Wiener Linien offices in U-Bahn stations, including Floridsdorf, Spittelau, Praterstern, Philadelphiabrücke, Landstrasse and Volkstheater. Purchase by credit card before you travel by calling 43 1 978 44 00 28.

Hundertwasserhaus
3, Kegelgasse, 43
☎ 413 93 95

Radsport Nussdorf
19, Donaupromenade
DDSG Anlegestelle
☎ 37 45 98

Riebl Sport
5, Schönbrunner Strasse, 63
☎ 544 75 34

Safe places to park your car

There are over twenty covered car parks in the city itself (1st district), but these are expensive (ATS40 for one hour) and there's still insufficient capacity. If you prefer to park in the road, there are limited parking zones in 1st, 4th, 5th, 6th, 7th, 8th and 9th districts, operating Mon.-Fri. 9am-7pm. You need to put a short-term parking ticket (*Kurzparkschein*) on the windscreen inside your vehicle. You can buy these tickets at tobacconists, railway stations and public transport ticket offices, and they cost ATS6 for 30 minutes, ATS12 for 60 minutes and ATS18 for 90 minutes. If your hotel is in the 4th, 5th, 6th, 7th , 8th or 9th districts and doesn't have a car parking facility, ask for a *Parkkarte* at reception (ATS50). This ticket will allow you to park all day in the designated zones. Note that the roads are patrolled frequently and fines are heavy. Be sure not to park on a winter's night in a road on which trams run – snow-clearing machines begin to work on the tracks at dawn, and you may find your vehicle in the pound.

The following indoor car parks are available: Parkhaus City, Wollzeile, 7; Parkgarage Am Hof (600 spaces); Garage Freyung (700 spaces); Tiefgarage Rathauspark, Dr Karl-Lueger-Ring; Tiefgarage Franz-Josefs-Kai, Morzinplatz, 1 (850 spaces); Garage Hoher Markt, Sterngasse, 5; Kärntnerstrasse Tiefgarage, Kärntnerstrasse, 51.

MAKING A TELEPHONE CALL

Austrian phone booths are usually dark green with a bright yellow roof and are simple to use. It's easier to make an international call with a phone card (*Telefon Wertkarte*), which you can purchase from post offices and tobacconists in denominations of ATS50, ATS100 and ATS200. From Vienna, dial 0044 for the UK, 00353 for Ireland, 001 for North America, 0061 for Australia and 0064 for New Zealand. The minimum charge for a 2-minute local call is ATS3 up to 50km/30 miles during the day or 5 minutes at night.

Do remember that the Austrian telephone system is one of the most expensive in the world. If you're planning to make lengthy phone calls, you can buy a 'telecard TNS', in denominations of ATS100, ATS200, ATS500 and ATS1000, at selected shops, one such being M Hirsch at Sterngasse, 2.

The code for Vienna when phoning from elsewhere in Austria is 0222, and from Vienna to other Austrian destinations you should dial the entire number including the prefix 0.

SENDING MAIL

The main post office (*Haupt Postamt*) is at Fleischmarkt,

19, U-Bahn Schwedenplatz, and is open 24 hours a day, seven days a week, along with post offices in the Westbahnhof, Sudbahnhof and Franz-Josefs Bahnhof. Others are open Mon.-Fri. 8am-noon, 2-6pm. Stamps (*Briefmarken*) can also be purchased at tobacconists and cost ATS6.50 for a postcard within the EU. A postcard to anywhere else in the world costs ATS13. Post takes about three to four days to reach the UK, five days the US and a week to ten days Australia and New Zealand.

CHANGING MONEY

You can change money at banks, which are generally open Mon.-Fri. 8am-12.30pm, 1.30-3pm, with late closing on Thursdays at 5.30pm. Outside these hours, you can change money at a *Wechselstube* (bureau de change), which can be found in railway stations and at the airport. There is also a *Changeomat* at Stephansplatz, but for the best rates and lowest commission it's advisable to withdraw cash (large sums at a time) from cash machines. Check with your bank before you leave for relevant charges.

Tourist Offices

The main tourist information point in Vienna is at the offices of the Vienna Tourist Board (*Wiener Tourismusverband*). Its general office is open Mon.-Fri. 8am-4pm, and is on Obere Augartenstrasse, 40, tel 211 14. There's also a branch in the heart of the city at Kärntnerstrasse, 38, which is open every day 9am-6pm, tel 513 88 92, but this is due to move to Albertinaplatz, 1, tel 211 140, in July/August 2000.

Guided Tours

Walks

The *Wiener Spaziergänge* leaflet has information about guided tours around the city, which normally last about 90 minutes and cost ATS150 and are in the company of a local specialist or official guide. You don't need to book ahead, just turn up at the appointed hour and meeting point specified in the leaflet (available from tourist information offices ☎ 894 53 63). A different world will unfold, including the dark occult secrets of the Court, the history of the Jewish citizens and underground Vienna. Do note that the price excludes entry charges to the sights and monuments themselves.

Bus tours

Vienna Sightseeing Tours, ☎ 712 46 830, runs a variety of guided tours, including the city by night, the Vienna woods and a tour following in the footsteps of Sissi. They take between 75 minutes (ATS220) and four hours (from ATS390) and leave from Wien-Mitte at 9.30am and 2.30pm. A more original way of seeing the city is to take the *Vienna Line hop-on hop-off*, which stops at the Opera, Prater, Belvedere and many other places. You can get on and off as many times as you like during a two-day consecutive period. It costs ATS250, and for more information ☎ 712 46 83-0 or visit the offices at Stelzhamergasse, 4/11.

Useful numbers

Emergency phone numbers

Fire ☎ 122

Police ☎ 133

Ambulance ☎ 144

SOS Doctor ☎ 141

Chemist ☎ 1550

Dentist ☎ 512 20 78

Road emergency

Arbö ☎ 123

Öamtc ☎ 120

Lost and found

Fundamt (head office) 9, Wasagasse, 22 ☎ 313 44 92 14

UK Embassy

3, Jauresgasse, 12 A-1030 Wien ☎ 716 13

Sites and Monuments

Museums are closed on Monday, Tuesday and public holidays (1 Jan., Easter Monday, 1 May, 1 Nov. and 25 Dec.). Entry charges range from ATS45-95. Students, children and pensioners receive discounts, and some museums have combined tickets, allowing access to more than one place at attractive prices. At the Kunsthalle, the *Kombikarte* is valid for exhibitions at the Museumsquartier and Treitlstrasse. The pass for the Lipizzaner Museum also entitles you to see the morning demonstration at the famous equestrian school.

Between the Cathedral and the Synagogue

If you walk from Stephansdom (nicknamed '*Steffl*') to the synagogue (*Stadttempel*), you'll get a good sense of how the city looked in the Middle Ages. The cathedral is the largest Gothic building in Vienna and its greatest symbol. The synagogue is concealed from the street (as decreed by the culturally repressive Josef II), and is hidden inside another building. Between the two buildings is a string of shops.

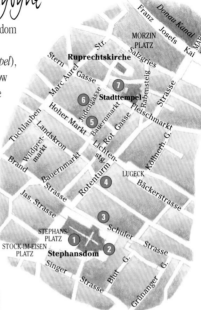

❶ Stephansdom

Stephansplatz
☎ 515 52 30
Open every day 6am-10pm
Organ concerts May-Nov.
Information from the tourist office.

Under the multi-coloured tiles on the steep roof of the cathedral are hidden treasures that give you an impression of the wealth of Vienna during the 16th and 17th centuries. Tobias Pock's high altar is well worth seeing, as is the carved stone pulpit by Anton Pilgram, with its portraits of the four fathers of the Christian church, its filigree work and its salamanders and toads, symbolising good and evil. The sculptor signed his work by showing himself peering from

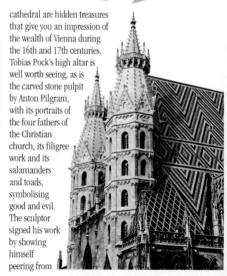

a window, and he can be seen again peeping out below his other work, the organ casing.

❷ Haas & Haas★★★
Stephansplatz, 4
☎ 512 97 70
Open Mon.-Fri. 9am-6pm, Sat. 9am-5pm.

Next to the tea room, in which you should try the Japanese *gykuro tanabe*, the South African *rooibos* or the incredible *jasmin imperial dragon pearl* from Guandong, you'll find yourself at Madame Haas' emporium, with its wonderful selection of coffees, biscuits and fruit tarts. The pastry cook here is a skilled craftsman, and there's a delightful garden attached, and orange pots-pourris are for sale as reminders of this lovely place. Try to fit in a visit.

❸ Metzger★
Stephansplatz, 7
☎ 512 34 33
Open Mon.-Fri. 9am-6pm, Sat. 9am-noon.

Question: when is a loaf of bread not a loaf of bread? Answer: when it's a candle. At Metzger's shop you'll find candles in

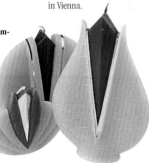

every conceivable shape and colour. He's the king of candles and a man who only has eyes for his bees. Wax lyrical at his creations — you are unlikely to find another shop that can hold a candle to this.

❹ Bizi★
Rotenturmstraße, 4
☎ 513 37 05
Open Mon.-Sun. 11am-11.30pm.

The main attraction of this enormously popular, very central and amazingly cheap café, is its mezzanine, where at any time of day and under subtle lighting, you can enjoy a four seasons pizza, plate of steamed vegetables or bowl of homemade pasta. It's the best of the many branches of 'Bizi' in Vienna.

❺ Ankeruhr★★
Hoher Markt, 10-11.

Pause in front of the glorious Jugendstil Ankeruhr, a heavily gilded clock designed by Frankz Matsch in 1914, where each

❻ BERMUDA-DREIECK (BERMUDA TRIANGLE)★
Ruprechtsplatz, Seitenstettengasse, Rabensteig.

Since the 1980s this area has been called the 'Bermuda Triangle' because there are so many bars and restaurants you could get lost forever. During the day tourists rather than revellers come to see the narrow streets, the city's oldest church (Ruprechtskirche) and the *Stadttempel* (synagogue), which is the only one to have survived *Kristallnacht* in 1938.

hour an automaton representing a key figure in Vienna's history shuffles across the clock dial. At noon the crowds gather to watch all twelve figures move across, accompanied by rather mournful music. Try and spot Marcus Aurelius, Charlemagne, Haydn, and Maria Theresa. In December there are Christmas carols at 5pm and 6pm.

Around the Graben: exclusive luxury

It all started in the Middle Ages, when the Graben (meaning ditch), originally the moat around the Roman camp, was filled in so that, much later, luxurious houses could be built. There are exclusive shops still sporting the *kaiserlich und königlich* emblem (Imperial and Royal) as if they were still supplying the Habsburg emperors. In between the old-fashioned stores are newer and bolder buildings, and interesting jewellery shops designed by Hans Hollein.

❸ Trzesniewski★
Dorotheergasse, 1
☎ 512 32 91
Open Mon.-Fri. 8.30am-7.30pm, Sat. 9am-5pm.

This is a real Viennese institution, a minimalist sandwich bar serving wonderful slices of rye bread topped with free-range eggs,

❶ Haas-Haus★★
Stock-im-Eisen-Platz, 4.

This building was highly controversial when it was unveiled in 1990. Designed by the architect Hans Hollein, it's an asymmetrical construction in metal-coated glass and marble with a protruding turret. There's a mini-shopping centre inside and a restaurant with a panoramic view on the seventh floor.

❷ Palais Equitable (Equitable Plaza)★★
Stock-im-Eisen-Platz, 3.

Built in the 1890s and recently restored, the Palais Equitable is a perfect example of the taste of the Viennese establishment. It has a highly ornate vestibule with a magnificent staircase and lots of marble and wrought iron, together with a glass-roofed courtyard.

8 Naglergasse★★

If you've had enough of the luxurious shops in the Graben, try the more intimate pedestrianised street called the Naglergasse, with its preserved Baroque facades decorated with cherubs. Here you can do more relaxed shopping and then have a quick drink at a *Bierlokal* (no. 13) or rustic *Stadtheisl* (no. 21). The latter also happens to be the starting-point for underground tours of Vienna.

The original museum was closed in 1938, reopened in 1989 and recently totally refurbished. It houses a bookshop and the Teitelbaum Café, where you can enjoy a tasty hot chocolate and a delicious strudel.

5 Pestsäule (Plague Column)★
Stephansplatz.

At the end of the plague epidemic that had claimed the lives of tens of thousands of citizens, Leopold 1 vowed to erect a commemorative column in the middle of the square. Johann Bernhard Fischer von Erlach, the creator of many Baroque buildings, designed the column, on which the Plague, in the form of an old hag,

is being burnt by Faith and a cherub.

6 Peterskirche (St Peter's Church)★★
Petersplatz.

This is one of Vienna's finest Baroque churches, a modest imitation of St Peter's in Rome, occupying a small

square of its own. There's a dazzling pulpit by Matthias Steinl, a recently restored fresco on the dome of The Assumption of the Virgin Mary by Johann Michael Rottmayr and a magnificent monument, designed by Lorenzo Matielli, depicting St John of Nepomuk being thrown off Prague's Charles Bridge. It's said that the Empress Elisabeth would spend many a quiet moment in front of this work of art.

7 Demel★★★
Kohlmarkt, 14
☎ 535 17 17
Open every day 10am-7pm.

Did Elisabeth spend a quiet moment in Peterskirche before she bought her favourite chocolates from Demel or afterwards? History doesn't tell us. This wonderful establishment was appointed imperial and royal confectioners in 1786 and its famous Kaffee-Konditorei dates from 1888, with a lavish interior restored in the 1930s. It now belongs to a German bank, but the *Linzertorte* remains delicious and deliveries are made worldwide. Check out their website for more information: www.demel.at.

salami and smoked fish. You eat standing up and wash it all down with a glass of beer. There's another branch at Mariahilferstrasse, 95.

4 Jüdisches Museum (Jewish Museum)★★★
Dorotheergasse, 11
☎ 535 04 31
Open Sun.-Fri. 10am-6pm, Thu. 10am-8pm
Entry charge.

This fascinating museum is housed halfway up in the Palais Eskeles and is both moving and instructive.

Kärntnerstrasse

The Kärntnerstrasse lies along the old road that led to the province of Corinthia (Kärnten) and on to the port of Trieste. It's still the main shopping street in the city centre and merchants and hoteliers have prospered here since the 12th century. Today the street is pedestrianised and a little less luxurious than at the beginning of World War I, but it's worth strolling round the adjacent streets between the Neuer Markt and Franziskanerplatz.

❶ Dorotheum★
Dorotheergasse, 17
☎ 515 60-0
Open Mon.-Fri.10am-6pm, Sat. 9am-6pm.

This is the city's premier auction house, from which the street gets its name, and you'll find almost everything for sale, including imperial chandeliers, Gallé vases, uniforms, weapons and helicopters. The auctions usually start at 2pm and a timetable can be obtained on the spot or from their website at www.dorotheum.com.

❷ Theatermuseum★
Lobkowitzplatz, 2
☎ 512 88 00
Open Tue.-Sun.10am-5pm, Wed. 10am-9pm.

The museum of Austrian theatre is housed in the Palais Lobkkowitz (1687), which is worth a visit in itself. Next to the Eroicasaal, where Beethoven's Third Symphony had its première in 1804, is a small room devoted to the puppets made by Richard Teschner (1879-1948).

❸ Kaisergruft★★
Neuer Markt
☎ 512 68 53 12
Open every day 9.30am-4pm
Entry charge.

The Habsburgs had the 'privilege' of being dissected after death, and their remains were then divided between the Stephansdom (entrails), the

Augustinerkirche (heart) and the crypt in the Capuchin church at Kaisergruft, where the remains of 139 Habsburgs lie, from Anne (who died in 1618) to Zita (who departed this world in 1989). Don't miss the vault of Empress Maria Theresa, which takes the form of an impressive bed covered in Rococo decorations.

4 Donnerbrunnen★
Neuer Markt.

Maria Theresa disliked this fountain intensely, though it's one of the most beautiful in Vienna. It was designed by Georg Raphael Donner in the Baroque style, but the Empress was shocked by the nudity of the four figures representing the tributaries of the Danube (the Enns, March, Ybbs and Traun). She had them removed in 1770, but they were returned in 1801 and finally replaced by bronze copies in 1873.

5 Steffl★
Kärntnerstrasse, 19
☎ 514 31 0
Open Mon.-Fri. 9.30am-7pm, Sat. 9.30am-5pm.

This department store has recently been renovated and now has an external lift to service its many floors. Perfume and jewellery are on the ground floor and books are on the top floor, where there's also a memorial to Mozart, who died in a building on this site in 1791. His home was on the ground floor on th side nearest Rauhensteingasse. However, there's no café, and the planned Planet Hollywood site is now a music store.

6 Gigerl★★
Blumenstockgasse, 2
☎ 513 44 31
Open every day from 11am.

Gigerl is a *Stadtheuriger,* a wine tavern located near the centre of the city rather than in the outer suburbs. According to an age-old tradition, a bunch of evergreen branches hangs outside when it's open. The buffet here is self-service and there are many hot and cold dishes to choose from to accompany your wine tasting. Enjoy the light, fresh taste of the year's most recent harvest and unwind in the midst of the hustle and bustle of the city.

7 BALLGASSE 4★★★
☎ 513 53 60, 513 13 31 or 512 05 75
Open Mon.-Fri. 11am-6pm, Sat. 11am-3pm.

This house was built around an interior courtyard in 1780 and is one of the jewels of the old town. It was restored in 1998, and today has studios, workshops and galleries. Here the Hegenbart family continues to restore furniture and mirrors, Christian Köhler exhibits his jewellery and Andreas Franek his lovely lamps.

Around the Palais Ferstel

Long ago this was one of the most elegant and aristocratic areas in Vienna, and today you can see the evidence of this in the Baroque façades of the Harrach, Batthyány-Schönborn and Kinsky palaces. The Palais Ferstel has long been home to the Café Central where Leo Bronstein (aka Leon Trotsky) spent many an hour – quite a contrast to its former inhabitants.

❶ Café Central★★★

Herrengasse, 14
☎ 533 37 63 26
Open Mon.-Sat. 8am-10pm.

This very beautiful café is housed in the Palais Ferstel. It was renovated in 1986 but was definitely at the height of its popularity at the turn of the century, when the city's intellectuals from the literary and political worlds would meet in its Gothic vaults.

Today's customers are more likely to be tourists, but you can still enjoy a *Palatschinke* (pancake) with apricots.

❷ Am Hof★

Hof means 'royal court' as well as 'courtyard', and this large square was named in medieval times, when the Babenberg family had their headquarters here. In the 12th century Jasomirgott Babenberg, the first duke

of Austria, chose this site to build his home. Today the enormous Baroque façade of the Jesuit church (*Kirche am Hof*), built in 1662 by Carlo Antonio Carlone, dominates the square with the imposing *Mariensäule* (Marian Column). Its cherubs do battle with a lion, dragon,

serpent and basilisk, representing the war, plague, hunger and heresy that threatened Vienna.

❸ Kurrentgasse★★★

This small street is lined with 18th-century houses and is one of the most attractive in Vienna. The buildings are painted in a delicate rose

colour and decorated with lovely statues. It opens onto the Judenplatz, the heart of the medieval Jewish ghetto (1294-1421), where the remains of a synagogue were recently excavated.

❹ Sankt Urban★
Am Hof, 11
☎ 532 28 35
Open Mon.-Fri. 9am-7pm,
Sat. 10am-2pm.

The Gottardis are passionate about wine and, with classical music playing softly in the background, will offer you a Chardonnay from their own vineyard in the Italian Tyrol, a Wachau vintage (Prager) and a popular wine from the Neusiedlersee (Schindler).

❺ Kunstforum★
Freyung, 8
☎ 532 06 44
Open every day 10am-6pm,
Wed. 10am-9pm
Entry charge.

Since 1989, the Austrian Bank has been holding exhibitions of art from the 19th and 20th centuries in the Kunstforum. Some of them have been quite general, including 'The masterpieces of the Guggenheim', others specific, such as those dedicated to the Expressionist painters, Emil Nolde and Ernst-Ludwig Kirchner.

❻ Museum im Schottenstift (Museum of the Monastery of Scots)★
Freyung, 6
☎ 534 98 60
Tue.-Sat. 10am-5pm, Sun. noon-5pm
Entry charge.

The sombre façade of this Benedictine monastery (built in fact to welcome Irish monks) hides two beautiful Baroque rooms and the

❽ DREIMÄDERLHAUS (HOUSE OF THE THREE YOUNG GIRLS)★

Schreyvogelgasse, 10

Rumour has it that this pretty home, with its Biedermeier garlands, was once Schubert's apartment, where he installed three lovers. It's a stone's throw from the Pasqualatihaus on Mölkerbastei, 8, where Beethoven composed three symphonies, his string quartet op. 59 and his only opera, *Fidelio*.

monastery's art collection, mostly 17th- and 18th-century Dutch and German still lifes and landscapes.

❼ Demmers Teehaus★★
Mölkerbastei, 5
☎ 533 59 95
Open Mon.-Fri. 10am-6pm.

In these elegant tearooms, designed by the architect Luigi Blau in 1981, you can taste 150 different types of tea as well as some delicious house specialities.

The Stubenviertel

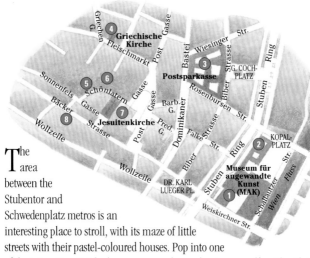

The area between the Stubentor and Schwedenplatz metros is an interesting place to stroll, with its maze of little streets with their pastel-coloured houses. Pop into one of the interesting *Beisl*, where you can relax and enjoy yourself until midnight. Whatever you do, don't miss the Austrian Museum of Applied Art, known simply as the MAK, where you can see art ranging from the Romanesque right up to the modern day.

❶ Museum für angewandte Kunst/MAK (Museum of Applied Art)★★★

Stubenring, 5
☎ 711 36 0
Open Tue.-Sun. 10am-6pm, Thu. 10am-9pm
Entry charge.

Founded in the 1860s by Rudolf von Eitelberger, this museum houses one of Vienna's most enjoyable and eclectic collections. Its renovation was completed in 1993, and each room was individually designed. In the Jugendstil room there's a silhouetted exhibition of chair design over the last hundred years, including pieces by Otto Wagner, Adolf Loos and Thonet.

❷ Mak-Café★★

☎ 714 01 21
Tue.-Sun. 10am-2pm.

The interactive exhibits in the MAK can sometimes be quite exhausting, so stop for refreshment in the trendy MAK café, with its wonderful high ceilings, designed by Hermann Czech. The food is Mediterranean in style and quite pricey, but this is definitely one of the cafés in which to be seen. It's a great place to go for a spot of coffee and and culture (*Kaffee und Kunst*).

❸ Postsparkasse (Postal Savings Bank)★★★
Georg-Coch-Platz, 2.

The PSK is one of the great works of Otto Wagner, who, from 1904-1906, used a new material – aluminium – to hold the grey marble slabs in place and form the curved ceiling. You can buy copies of objects designed by Wagner and his pupils from the ticket office on Bibergasse, open Mon.-Fri. 8am-3pm (5.30pm on Thursday).

❽ SPECHT★
Bäckerstraße, 12
☎ 512 26 37
Open every day 5pm-1am.

Under the medieval arches of this tavern you can enjoy a glass of good local wine or even something special, such as Falkenstein, while munching on specialities, including *Wiener Mariellenknödel mit Nussbrösel*. You can enjoy Viennese music on a Friday, Saturday or Sunday. A fun place to come.

❹ Griechische Kirche★
Fleischmarkt, 13.

Enter for a moment or two into the world of the Greeks in this Orthodox church, built by Theophil von Hansen in 1861 and gleaming with gold from Byzantium. You can attend a service on Sunday, 10am-noon.

❺ Schönlaterngasse (Beautiful Lantern Lane)★★
This is a charming, romantic cobbled street, lined with attractive medieval houses,

including Basiliskenhaus (no. 7) and the old smithy (*Alte Schmiede*) (no. 9), now an art gallery. Robert and Clara Schumann lived at no. 7a.

❻ Galerie im Heiligen- kreuzerhof★
Entry via Schönlaterngasse, 5
☎ 513 20 53
Open Tue.-Thu. 11am- 1pm, 2-6pm, Fri. 2-6pm.

This is one of Vienna's secret treasures, an inner courtyard belonging to the Cistercian abbey of Heiligenkreuz. Inside is an antique shop run by Herr Dürrer, which is full of Russian icons, Jugendstil furniture, pretty rustic cupboards and Austrian art.

❼ Jesuitenkirche★★
Dr. Ignaz-Seipel-Platz, 1.

The Jesuit church was begun in 1627, when the Jesuits were at the height of their power and influence. It's also known as the Universitätskirche (University Church), and Andra Pozzo designed its extremely ornate, Baroque interior in the early 18th century. Its spiral columns in red and green marble and trompe-l'oeil dome make it one of Vienna's most impressive Baroque churches. It's certainly a wonderful example of the artistic fever that gripped Vienna in the early 1700s.

Hofburg: the museum district

The vast complex of the 'Court Palace' housing 18 buildings and over 20 courtyards, was the Austrian monarchy's seat of power for over six centuries. Even if you manage to visit only a few of its 2,600 rooms, you'll get a good idea of how Vienna looked under imperial rule. What's more, three of the departments of the exceptional Kunsthistorisches Museum (Art History Museum), also known as KHM, are housed in the Hofburg.

forced to install bronze flower-boxes, to be filled with greenery all year round, in order to temper the appearance of a 'house without eyebrows' (as Franz Josef had described it). It's now a bank with an exhibition area.

❸ C. Bühlmayer★
Michaelerplatz, 6
☎ 533 10 49
Open Tue.-Thu. 9am-6pm, Sat. 9am-1pm.

❶ Café Griensteidl★
Michaelerplatz, 2
☎ 535 26 93
Open every day 8am-midnight.

Since your day will have focused heavily on the Habsburgs, order a 'Maria Theresa' in this resurrected literary café — a double moka with a hint of orange liqueur and a spoonful of whipped cream. Demolished in 1897, it was nicknamed *Café Grossenwahn* ('Delusions of Grandeur').

❷ Loos Haus
Michaelerplatz, 3
Open Mon.-Wed. 8am-3pm, Thu. 8am-5.30pm.

When the Loos Haus was built in 1911, it caused uproar, and the architect Adolf Loos was

This studio is hidden at the end of the Michaelerhof, and it's here that Herr Haider renovates old mirrors, adding gold leaf, polishing with agate and creating wonderful effects. It's a great place to buy picture frames.

4 Lipizzaner Museum★

Reitschulgasse, 2
☎ 526 41 84 30
Open every day 9am-6pm
Entry charge.

You can either attend a morning training session at the riding school

(*Morgenarbeit*), Tue.-Sat. 10am-noon (mid Jan.-June, late Aug.-mid Dec.) or why not trot across to the Lippizanner Museum and see the antique horse tack, uniforms and videos. While you're here, have a quick look at the horses in their stalls if you have time.

5 Nationalbibliothek (National Library)★★★

Josefsplatz, 1
☎ 534 100
Open Mon.-Sat. 10am-4pm (until 2pm in winter), Sunday 10am-1pm
Entry charge.

The National Library is Austria's largest working library, and the Prunksaal (Grand Hall) is a huge Baroque room by Fischer von Erlach (father and son), with pillars, statues of Habsburg rulers and a magnificent fresco on the dome. It contains 200,000 books together with maps, globes and manuscripts.

6 Palmenhaus★★★

Burggarten
☎ 533 10 33
Open every day 10am-2pm.

Thanks to Andreas Bohm and Roland Traunbauer, the citizens of Vienna can now dine among the palms in this stylish modern greenhouse café. After a visit to the Hofburg, treat yourself to a warm goat's cheese salad and some grilled fish with a glass of Grüner Veltliner (a white, dry and fruity wine). This café is inexpensive and it is well worth a visit.

7 Neue Burg★★

Heldenplatz
☎ 525 240 or 534 300
Open Wed.-Mon. 10am-4pm (10am-6pm Jan.-Mar.)
Entry charge.

This was the last wing of the Hofburg to be built and houses the **Hofjagd-und Rüstkammer** (Court Hunting and Arms Collection), with its wonderful collection of armour, and the **Museum für Völkerkunde** (Museum of Ethnology), with a very wide-ranging collection including Japanese masks, Hawaiian artefacts from Captain Cook's Expedition and Aztec headdresses.

8 KUNSTHISTORISCHES MUSEUM (ART HISTORY MUSEUM)★★★

Maria-Theresien-Platz
☎ 525 24 0
Open Tue.-Sun. 10am-6pm (Thu. until 9pm)
Entry charge.

Visiting the KHM, with its wonderful exhibitions, is a pure delight. Don't miss 'Susanna and the Elders' by Tintoretto (room 3), large 18th-century views of Vienna by Bernardo Belotto (room 7), and Bruegel's 'Hunters in the Snow' (room 10). The building itself is lavishly decorated with a shining foyer and staircase.

Spittelberg: romantic and bohemian

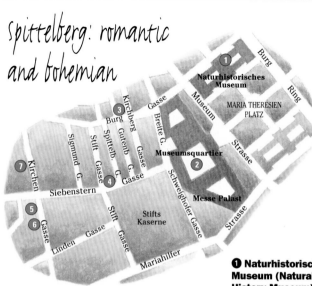

This area of Vienna is at its most attractive when covered in snow. It used to be a working-class quarter and red-light district, full of artisans and soldiers, whereas today it's the favourite haunt of the intelligentsia, architects, tourists and the very trendy. It has a craft market on Saturdays and lovely restored Baroque and Biedermeier buildings.

❶ Naturhistorisches Museum (Natural History Museum)★★★
Maria-Theresien-Platz
☎ 521 77 0

Open Wed.-Mon. 9am-6pm Entry charge.

Every Viennese child knows the Natural History Museum and its most famous exhibit, the 25,000-year-old Venus of Willendorf. What you see is in fact a replica of the small fertility symbol. If this doesn't move you, why not venture into room 24, where there are wonderful butterflies, or room 28, where there's a giant Japanese crab and a crocodile from the Ganges.

❷ Museumsquartier★
Museumsplatz, 1
☎ 521 89 0, 522 76 13 or 524 48 0.
Open every day 10am-6pm (Thu. until 10pm)
Entry charge.

The Museumsquartier is set to be the largest cultural complex in Austria, rivalling the Pompidou Centre in Paris. It has been the cause of lively popular debate, but the exhibitions and interactive museums are already installed in the former imperial stables. Pick up a free plan at the main entrance.

❸ Das Möbel★★★
Burggasse, 10
☎ 524 94 97
Open every day noon-midnight.

The Viennese are good at café concepts. In *Das Möbel* (The Furniture) they've come up with the idea of trying out the chairs while enjoying a cup of coffee. You can eat here, too, and at 6pm on Tuesday they serve cocktails, so why not have a Pina Colada on a bicycle seat? You can pay for the coffee and chair or just the coffee.

❹ Galerie Holzer★
Spittelberggasse, 1
☎ 523 72 18
Open Mon.-Fri. 10am-6pm, Sat. 10am-5pm.

With his passion for Jugendstil and Art Deco furniture and fittings, Werner Holzer has filled his antique shop with beautiful lacquered maple cabinets, cream vases with black patterns and chairs with small square holes, all reminders of the powerful artistic movement that took Vienna by storm. There are more showrooms at Kirchengasse, 30, and Siebensterngasse, 32-34.

❺ Shultz★★
Siebensterngasse, 31
☎ 522 91 20
Open Mon.-Sat. 9am-10pm, Sun. 4pm-2am.

Shultz is a fun daytime bar, Californian in style, where excellent daiquiris are served by the extremely friendly staff. You can have a snack, too, such as a bagel with roast beef and herb cheese. The music is good too.

❻ Se'Stelle★
Kirchengasse, 21
☎ 524 04 17
Open every day 9am-midnight.

This Italian restaurant is quite the opposite of a typical Napolitan trattoria.

❼ Chactun★★
Kirchengasse, 25
☎ 524 08 09
Open Mon.-Fri. noon-7.30pm, Sat. 11am-5pm.

It's not enough for Marc Chactun to encourage young designers by selling their creations in his shop, including shirts by Christoph Nardeaux and jackets with holograms, fluorescent strips or plastic epaulettes. He also organises parties, and you can find the dates and venues on flyers and at their website: www.chactun.at.

The atmosphere here is positively relaxed, the cuisine unusually light and it is all served in a large, airy space, designed by the renowned architect Heinz Lutter in wood and glass. You can have *tramezzini* at any hour, and at lunchtime you can opt for a three-course set meal for ATS110, featuring

fettucine and grilled scampi with saffron. Be sure not to miss the selection of fruit juices from the Preiss orchards, which really are truly delicious.

Mariahilf: a shopper's paradise

Mariahilferstrasse is the longest shopping street in Austria. It stretches for more than 2km/1 mile from the KHM in the east to the Westbahnhof in the west, with over six hundred shops, offering every kind of item imaginable. It's also home to the *Kaiserliches Hofmobiliendepot* (Imperial Furniture Collection), a cross between a museum and a junk warehouse. Most of Vienna's department stores are on this street.

❶ Rag★
Mariahilferstrasse, 17
☎ 581 30 06
Open Mon.-Fri. 9.30am-6pm, Sat. 9.30am-5pm.

This is a very cool shop selling the trendiest streetwear labels. It's a favourite with young hip hop and skateboard fans, who come here for their jeans, oversized T-shirts and Caterpillars.

❷ Peek & Cloppenburg★
Mariahilferstrasse, 26-30
☎ 52 56 10
Open Mon.-Fri. 9am-9pm, Sat. 9am-5pm.

There's nothing like an escalator ride through the heart of the Mariahilf department stores to make you feel like a shopaholic.

Each shop has its own special attraction – Leiner (no. 18) for furniture, Gerngross (nos. 38-48) for fruit and vegetables and P & C for fashion. Diesel clothes for men are in the basement, Tommy Hilfiger on the first floor and DKNY on the second.

❸ Mariahilferkiche★
Mariahilferstrasse, 55.

The other advantage of this wide avenue is that you can appreciate the size, composition and charm of this large Baroque façade, which was built between 1686 and 1689 by Sebastiano

Carlone. It has retained its splendid organs and a lovely balustrade..

❹ Komolka★
Mariahilferstrasse, 58
☎ 523 71 84
Open Mon.-Fri. 10am-6.30pm, Sat. 10am-5pm.

At this shop you can browse through rolls of material on three floors, of every conceivable colour and fabric, and at amazing prices. You'll find Ungaro crêpe, Versace and Cerruti Jacquard, Lurex jersey, and even a bright fuchsia brocade that will certainly get you noticed when you go home.

❺ Turek Workshop Company★★
Mariahilferstrasse, 60
☎ 523 97 55
Open Mon.-Fri. 9.30am-7pm, Sat. 9am-5pm.

Turek has become amazingly popular in Vienna, and not without reason. It has all the latest labels (Eastpak, Hugo and Kikwear), plus own brand gear at reasonable prices, and its G-Star denims and roomy Forest Nature jumpers have been big hits. There's also a café in which to relax, unwind, read the papers (and flyers with info about future clubbing events) and enjoy a sandwich, while keeping a keen eye on what's happening on the street.

❻ Skala★★
Neubaugasse, 8
☎ 523 96 63
Open Mon.-Sat. 5pm-2am.

If your idea of cooking is opening a tin,

and vegetables are something you have to eat rather than enjoy, then Skala is the place to convert you. Everything here is fresh, healthy and delicious. The menu changes daily and is excellent, the small garden is lovely and the staff are very friendly and helpful. What more could you ask for?

❼ KAISERLICHES HOFMOBILIENDEPOT ★★★

Andreasgasse, 7
☎ 524 33 570
Open every day 9am-5pm.

The Imperial Furniture Collection was established by Maria Theresa in 1747 to supply the furniture required by the Habsburgs for their palaces. It has over 650,000 items, including candelabras, wardrobes, lapis-lazuli cabinets and footrests, together with reconstructed period interiors. Have a look at Crown Prince Rudolf's Turkish boudoir lined with the carpets he acquired during his oriental trip in 1881.

Naschmarkt: behind the scenes at the market

This is the largest of Vienna's markets. It follows the old course of the river between Karlsplatz and Kettenbrückengasse and has been held on this site for over a hundred years. It has witnessed a good deal of controversy, including the erection of Otto Wagner's Art Nouveau buildings and the battles waged over the Kunsthalle.

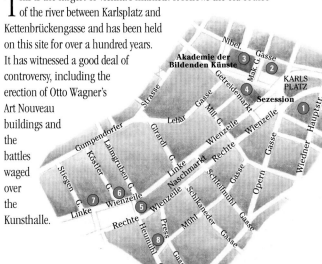

❶ Kunsthalle★
Treitlstrasse, 2
☎ 521 89 33
Open every day 10am-6pm(Thu. until 10pm)
Entry charge.

Also known as *Kunstschachtel* (Art Box), this controversial corrugated building by Adolf Krischanitz is a vast new arts venue and houses some unusual and interesting exhibitions of contemporary artists. The café is worth a visit, from where you can enjoy the architecture of the University library. There are some interesting events worth attending on Friday and Saturday evenings.

❷ Albertina★★
Makartgasse, 3
☎ 581 60 21
Open Tue.-Fri. 10am-6pm, Sat.-Sun. 10am-4pm
Entry charge.

Named after and founded by Albrecht, Duke of Saxony-Teschen, the Albertina was built in 1768. It's closed for restoration work until 2001, but temporary exhibitions are held in the Akademiehof in Makartgasse, 3. It has one of the world's largest collections of graphic art, including 50,000 drawings, etchings and watercolours, among them works by Dürer, Raphael, Rembrandt, Klimt and Schiele, together with a million and a half printed works.

❸ Akademie der Bildenden Künste (Academy of Fine Arts)★★
Schillerplatz, 3
☎ 588 16 225
Open Tue.-Sun. 10am-4pm
Entry charge.

The Academy of Fine Arts is housed in a neo-Renaissance building designed by Theophil Hansen (1871). There's an impressive collection of paintings, including works by Rembrandt, Van Dyck and Rubens. Don't miss 'The Last Judgement' by Hieronymus Bosch.

❹ Secession★★
Friedrichstrasse, 12
☎ 587 53 07
Open Tue.-Fri. 10am-6pm,
Sat.-Sun. 10am-4pm
Entry charge.

The headquarters of the Secession movement is in a wonderful Jugendstil building with a dome of gilded laurel leaves, known by locals as the 'golden cabbage'. It's the work of Joseph Maria Olbrich (1898), built as a reaction to the Ringstrasse's imposing and sterile architecture. Don't miss the 'Beethoven Frieze' in the basement,

painted by Klimt for an exhibition in 1902.

❺ Naschmarkt★★★
Wienzeile
Open Mon.-Fri. 6am-6.30pm, Sat. 4am-2pm.

Join the locals in this colourful market where many Viennese buy their fruit and vegetables. You'll hear every Central European language being spoken as you tour Turkish, Slav, Chinese and Arabian stalls. On Saturday

there's a flea market at the western end.

❻ Café Savoy★
Linke Wienzeile, 36
☎ 586 73 48
Open Mon.-Fri. 5pm-2am,
Sat. 9am-6pm, 9pm-2am.

Try to come here on a Saturday at the stroke of midday and enjoy a coffee or aperitif. Bargain-hunters from the Naschmarkt and flea

market come to revive themselves, antique dealers pop in for refreshment.

❼ Wienzeilehäuser★★★
Linke Wienzeile, 38 & 40
Köstlergasse, 1 & 3.

Otto Wagner constructed the metro station and these two Jugendstil buildings (1899), whose decorative features include golden medallions and rosebushes made of ceramic squares. Inside the buildings there are wonderful lift cages.

❽ FRANZ★★
Pressgasse, 29
☎ 585 25 57

Open every day 10am-2pm.

With its brick and wood interior, Franz is not only a friendly bar where you can have a tasty salad between midday and 2pm, it's also the only place in Vienna where late risers can have breakfast until 5pm. The 'mega breakfast' is made up of eggs, cheese and cold meats, muesli, fruit juice and all the coffee you can drink.

From the Ring to the Belvedere

A s soon as it was built, the Ringstrasse became a fashionable place to see and be seen in. People from all social strata would take an afternoon stroll along the road that climbs gently to the Belvedere. It became the favourite haunt of bankers, noblemen and ladies in mink coats. The palaces of the princes and dukes of Schwarzenberg, Wurtemberg and Savoie-Carignan are today impressive reminders of the Ring's former glory.

① Rosenkavalier★★
Kärntner Ring, 13
☎ 512 61 90
Open Mon.-Fri. 10am-7pm, Sat. 10am-5pm.

This florist on the ground floor of the Ringstrasse Galerie is worth the walk in itself. The flower arrangements are wonderfully colourful, making creative use of unusual pieces of wood and vegetation. In fact, everything you might dream of growing on your own balcony is here.

② Hotel Imperial★★★
Kärntner Ring, 16
☎ 501 10 0
F 501 10 410.

This hotel is considered to be amongst the most beautiful in the world and is certainly the most popular former palace in Vienna. It's also the official State Hotel (*Staatshotel*), where visiting dignitaries stay, one of its most famous former 'guests' being Hitler. If you go inside, make sure you look at the marble staircase. The cakes in the café are delicious, and the staff are resplendent in bow ties and white gloves.

③ Otto Wagner-Pavillon★★★
Karlsplatz
Open Tue.-Sun. 9am-12.15pm, 1-4.30pm.

In 1894, the architect Otto Wagner was commissioned to design the stations, bridges and viaducts of the Viennese metro system. Just four years later, in collaboration with Josef Maria Olbrich, he completed the two stunning entrance pavilions for the now defunct Karlsplatz station. With their gold trimmings, sunflower motif

and wrought-iron structure, they became perfect examples of the new art movement, *Jugendstil*.

❹ Karlskirche★★
Karlsplatz.

The Karlskirche is Vienna's finest Baroque church, presiding over the Karlsplatz with a rather eclectic mix of architectural features: a Neoclassical portico with two columns modelled on Trajan's Column in Rome, pagoda-style roof and Baroque side towers. Begun in 1716 by Johann Bernhard Fischer von Erlach and completed by his son Joseph Emanuel in 1739, it was dedicated to the

16th-century saint, Carlo Borromeo. Its russet, gold and white interior is serene and harmonious, and there's a stunning fresco by Johann Michael Rottmayr.

❺ Palais Schwarzenberg★★★
Schwarzenbergplatz, 9
☎ 79 84 51 56 00
Open every day 6.30-10am, noon-2.30pm, 6-10.30pm.

It would be hard to imagine a better place to enjoy pâté de fois gras or lobster in Chablis. If you can't afford to pay a king's ransom to stay in the hotel itself, a Baroque palace begun by Johann Lukas von Hildebrandt and completed by Fischer von Erlach, then treat yourself to a meal on the terrace of the lovely restaurant. There's a pretty park, which has largely been well preserved.

❻ Belvedere★★★
Rennweg, 6a
☎ 795 57 0

❼ Alpengarten (Alpine Garden)★★
Landstrasse Gürtel, 1
☎ 798 31 49

Open every day Apr.-Jul. 10am-6pm.

This small walled garden was founded in 1793. Escape the crowds that flock to Belvedere park and enjoy comparative tranquillity as you stroll between the statues and rockeries. Designed by Dominique Girard, the garden has heathers, shrubs and alpine flowers, including edelweiss, and is less strenuous than a mountain walk, but just as educational.

Open Tue.-Sun. 10am-5pm
Entry charge.

This was the home of Prince Eugéne of Savoy, Austria's greatest military leader. It's made up of two palaces, *Oberes Belvedere* (Upper Belvedere) and *Unteres Belvedere* (Lower Belvedere), both constructed by Hildebrandt. The former houses an art gallery, with works by Klimt (including 'The Kiss'), Schiele and Kokoschka. Lower Belvedere has retained more of its original Baroque décor and houses paintings from the medieval and Baroque periods.

Schönbrunn: the Austrian Versailles

Spend a day exploring Schönbrunn, the Habsburgs' summer residence built in 1696 by Fischer von Erlach, and take a walk in its lovely grounds. Visit the Palm House and the zoo, or simply wander along the Schlosspark's winding paths, enjoying the follies and ornamental pools. Access to the palace has more than a hint of the airport check-in about it, with rather strict departure times and points allocated for tours, but it still has great charm.

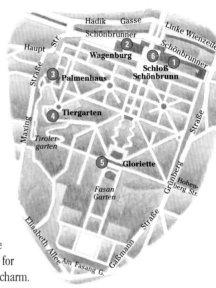

Don't miss the Great Gallery, which is a huge, long hall with gilded stucco and ceiling frescoes honouring the Habsburgs, or the Round Chinese Cabinet where Maria Theresa held secret meetings. As extra security, a table laden with food would rise up through a trapdoor in the floor, dispensing with the need for eavesdropping servants.

❷ Wagenburg★★★
☎ 877 32 44
Open every day Apr.-Oct. 9am-6pm, Nov.-Mar. Tue.-Sun. 10am-4pm
Entry charge.

The Wagenburg is full of 19th-century carriages used to transport the imperial family. The most spectacular of these are the coronation carriage of Franz Stephan and the

❶ Prunkräume★★★
☎ 813 13 239
Open every day Apr.-Oct. 8.30am-5pm, Nov.-Mar. 8.30am-4.30pm
Entry charge.

Not all of the 40 rooms open to the public are worth spending much time in, but the State Rooms are stunning.

carriage of Karl VI, painted by pupils of Rubens. The most moving is the tiny carriage designed for Napoloen's son, known as 'The Little Eagle', with mudguards shaped like eagle's wings and a bee motif, the Bonaparte family emblem.

❸ Palmenhaus (Palm House)★★
☎ 877 50 87 406
Open every day May-Sept. 9.30am-5.30pm, Oct.-Apr. 9.30am-4.30pm
Entry charge.

The Habsburgs financed many botanic expeditions to all four corners of the world from the 18th century onwards. Flowers and trees were brought back and housed in the Palm House, where today 4,000 plants flourish, amongst them the *aristolochia littoralis* (Dutchman's Pipe), with purple flowers and white spots (Section S3). This is a real jungle in the heart of the city.

❹ Tiergarten★
☎ 877 92 94 0
Open every day May-Sep. 9am-6.30pm, Oct.-Apr. 9am-4.30pm.

This zoo, the world's oldest, was established in the royal menagerie, where the imperial couple would have breakfast surrounded by animals in the *Frühstückspavillon des Kaisers*. Bored with plants, the Habsburgs began to collect animals instead, and you'll find all the usual suspects plus wolves, polar bears and giant tortoises. There's also the Tirolergarten and a large farmhouse from the Tyrol, complete with sheep, cows and horses. There's also a café serving Austrian food.

❺ Gloriette★★
☎ 879 13 11
Open every day 8am-dusk.

The neo-Classical Gloriette

❻WEIHNACHTSMARKT★★
Open 21 Nov.- 27 Dec.
Mon.-Fri. noon-8pm, Sat. & Sun. 10am-8pm,
Christmas Eve 10am-4pm.

The Christmas Market held in the palace courtyard every year is one of the most charming and authentic in Vienna. The choice is wonderful and the quality good, so take the opportunity to buy candles, wooden toys and tree decorations here, together with other Christmas provisions. Bask in the festive spirit.

presides over the park, celebrating the victory of the Habsburgs over the Prussians at the Battle of Kolin in 1757. There's also a café, where they serve exquisite pear and chocolate mousse tarts.

❼ Hietzinger Bräu★★
Auhofstrasse, 1
☎ 877 70 87 0
Open every day 11.30am-3pm, 6-10.30pm.

Opposite the legendary Dommayer restaurant, the Plachutta family café is a must on any gastronomic tour of Vienna. The food is delicious and the late 19th-century decor is very atmospheric. Keen carnivores should try the *Schulterscherzl* or *Hüferschwanzel* and other cuts of tender beef, served traditionally in copper vessels with soup and sliced bone marrow. It's an authentic gastronomic experience.

Alsergrund: home to intellectuals

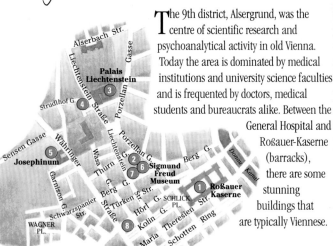

The 9th district, Alsergrund, was the centre of scientific research and psychoanalytical activity in old Vienna. Today the area is dominated by medical institutions and university science faculties and is frequented by doctors, medical students and bureaucrats alike. Between the General Hospital and Roßauer-Kaserne (barracks), there are some stunning buildings that are typically Viennese.

❶ Roßauer-Kaserne★★
Schlickplatz.

After the 1848 revolution, Vienna set about building barracks for its troops in double-quick time. The Roßauer-Kaserne is a red-brick construction, eclectic in style, that's part 'Windsor Castle', part Neo-Romantic and part mock-Gothic. It's currently used by the police.

❷ Blatt & Blüte★
Porzellangasse, 11
☎ 315 66 98
Open Mon.-Fri. 9am-7pm, Sat. 9am-5pm.

This is a really wonderful florist's, with an unusual monochrome interior and paintings that complement the colourful, inventive floral arrangements. The shop is a visual feast, and a delight for many of the senses.

❸ Palais Liechtenstein★★
Fürstengasse,1
☎ 317 69 00
Open Tue.-Sun. 10am-6pm
Entry charge.

The sumptuous summer palace, commissioned at the turn of the 17th century by the hugely wealthy Liechtenstein family, is now Vienna's Museum of Modern

Art (*Museum moderner Kunst*). The collection is scheduled to move to a new complex (Messeplatz) during the year 2000. The museum offers a wonderful opportunity to gaze at Pop Art (including the car by Cesar) in one of Vienna's most Baroque rooms with its ceiling painted by Andrea Puzzo. The rest of the collection is housed in the 20er Haus on Arsenalstrasse.

❹ Strudlhofstiege★
Liechtensteinstrasse.

When you emerge from the Palace, cast a glance at or even climb the Jugendstil staircase designed by Theodor Jager in 1910. The steps, with their balustrade and lamps, were the inspiration for a lengthy novel by Heimito von Doderer, much loved by many Viennese.

❺ Josephinum★★
Währinger Strasse, 25
☎ **403 21 54**
Open Mon.-Fri. 9am-3pm.
Entry charge.

The Josephinum, founded in 1785 by Josef II, houses an amazing collection of anatomical wax models (*Wächspräparate Sammlung*). These life-size human figures, partly dissected to show the nerves, muscles and veins of the body, were used to teach the future doctors and surgeons of the Austrian army. They're remarkably life-like (they were made by a group of Florentine sculptors), so be prepared! This is not for the faint-hearted.

❻ Sigmund-Freud-Museum★

Berggasse, 19
☎ **319 15 96**
Open every day 9am-4pm (in summer until 6pm)
Entry charge.

Today, pilgrims of Freud flock to this museum, which was both home and surgery to the author of 'The Interpretation of Dreams' for nearly fifty years. It was here that he received his patients, but, sadly, you won't be able to lie on his couch, as he took most of his possessions with him when he and his family were forced to flee to London in 1938. There's an exhibition of photographs with English captions.

❼ Ragusa★★
Berggasse, 15
☎ **317 15 77**
Open every day 11.30am-3pm, 6pm-midnight.

This is a fish and seafood restaurant run by Herr Stjepovic, who prepares delicious dishes of squid and scampi that will make you feel you can smell the Adriatic and see the sun shining in Dubrovnik. The wines are Croatian and reasonably priced.

❽ CAFÉ STEIN★★
Währinger Strasse, 6-8
☎ **319 72 41**
Open Mon.-Sat. 7am-1pm, Sun. 9am-1pm.

Eichinger and Knechtl's decor is complemented by the trendy student clientèle at this café which is just a stone's throw from the university. You can be connected to the Internet at the terminals inside, visit a few chat rooms or mingle on the terrace and enjoy tasty hot dishes (risotto, lamb curry and baked aubergine/eggplant) before heading for the nightclub. Good food, good atmosphere, good location.

Landstrasse: a place of fun and fantasy

If you've had enough of the Ringstrasse and its imposing palaces, head for the area between the Danube canal and the Landstrasser Hauptstrasse. It's Vienna's 3rd district and an attractive, if eclectic, place, where classical buildings rub shoulders with modernist architecture (Wittgensteinhaus). There's also an apartment block painted by a Viennese disciple of Gaudi, Friedensreich Hundertwasser, whose 'village' is now in the top four tourist attractions of Vienna.

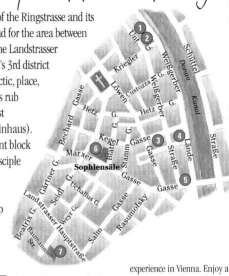

of St Barbara at Barnbach. The museum shop is full of T-shirts, scarves, postcards, calendars and posters. See below for information about the café housed here too.

❷ Café im Kunsthaus★★★
Untere Weißgerberstrasse, 14
☎ 712 04 97
Open every day 10am-midnight.

Pop into the café for a unique experience in Vienna. Enjoy a salad or bowl of broccoli soup in surroundings that are a mixture of 'The Jungle Book' and 'Alice in Wonderland', the bizarre and the odd, in the midst of wild vegetation. Your cup of coffee is about the only thing not attributed to Herr Hundertwasser. It's a pleasant place to relax for a moment.

❸ Hundertwasser-Haus★★★
Kegelgasse, 36-38

❶ Kunsthaus Wien★★
Untere Weißgerberstrasse, 13
☎ 712 04 91
Open every day 10am-7pm.

Hundertwasser also painted this housing block, which contains a gallery dedicated to his own paintings, photos and albums. You'll find scale models of his projects, including one of the church

This building was constructed by Peter Pelikan in 1985, based on designs by Hundertwasser. It seems to defy balance and order, in a higgledy-piggledy fashion, but each apartment in fact has a very precise colour and window design. The rent is very reasonable and you can even doodle on the walls. The 200 tenants have little to complain about except the number of tourists that come to look at their homes.

❹ Hummel★★
Untere Weißgerberlände, 522
☎ **718 24 68**
Open every day 9am-6pm.

If you can't make it to the warehouse in Kegelgasse, then pop into Beate Hummel's new shop just a stone's throw from Hundertwasser's 'village'. There's a good selection of wooden and cane furniture, together with boxes and other

unique items from the Sunda Islands. You'll find a host of ideas with which to decorate your home.

❺ Steirereck★★★
Rasumofskygasse, 2
☎ **713 31 68**
Open Mon.-Fri. noon-3pm, 7pm-midnight.

This is one of Vienna's finest restaurants and a favourite haunt of the city's many gourmets. It has all the attributes required to make it a success: a covered courtyard, excellent service, a very friendly wine waiter, delicious *foie gras,* a superb menu and wine list and not least, Helmut Österreicher, a chef who has won many awards. The lunch menu costs around ATS400, and the evening menu ATS900.

❻ Sophiensäle★
Marxergasse, 24
☎ **712 21 98 0 or 06 64 162 70 31.**

The former opulent imperial ballroom now welcomes a less formal clientèle, who come here to relax and dance to different rhythms, depending on the day of the week.

Modelling contests are also held here. It's the temple of clubbing, the like of which is hard to find elsewhere.

❼ BIEDERMEIER IM SÜNNHOF★★★
Landstrasser Hauptstrasse, 28
☎ **716 710 or 716 71 503.**

This is a charming hotel located in a narrow street classified as a historic site, the Sünnhof. Everything is from the Biedermeier period, including the kitchen, the café, the cherry wood furniture and the interior, which is pink and lime green. A double room in high season ATS2500, including breakfast.

On the banks of the Danube

The Donau or Danube, the great and almost mythical river of Central Europe, divides into four in Vienna, the Old Danube, the New Danube, the Canal and the river itself. Between the branches lie islands that have been made into parks. The Donau Island (*Donauinsel*) was created when the New Danube was cut in the 1970s and the locals flock to its 42km/26miles of beaches. From here there's a view over the skyline of 'New Vienna' on the east bank, with its latest addition, the huge Millennium Tower.

❶ DDSG★★
Schwedenbrücke
☎ 727 50 451/454

In the summer months, April to October, the DDSG 'Hundertwasser Tour' takes you on a boat trip on the Danube, leaving from the Canal. It includes the locks designed in 1898 by Otto Wagner, the Spittelau plant painted by Hundertwasser, and the UNO City complex (Vienna International Centre). The trip costs around ATS200 per person.

❷ Prater★
Open every day 8am–1pm.

You really need at least a couple of days to explore this large tract of land, the former imperial hunting ground, which is a favourite spot of the locals. It was opened up to the public in 1766 by Josef II and now includes a fairground with a popular giant ferris wheel (*Riesenrad*), racetracks, a miniature railway, a trade fair centre, sports stadia and a long avenue lined with chestnut trees. If you get peckish you can choose one of the many Wurst (sausage) stands or have roast pig at the famous Schweizer Haus.

❸ Augarten★
Open every day 6am–dusk.

This is a green haven of tranquillity, where locals come for picnics, to play

boules or to walk the dog. The Porcelain Museum (Wiener Porzellanmanufaktur), also in the grounds, is open Mon.-Fri. 9am-6pm, Sat. 9am-noon, tel 21 12 40. The factory was founded in 1718 and housed in the former garden pavilion. You can have a guided tour of the museum at 9.30am, which takes you through the various stages of production and types of glaze involved in making porcelain.

1979, after New York and Geneva. You have to present your identity card/passport in order to gain entry, but if you prefer not to go inside, just gaze at the reflections of the sunset in the 24,000 windows of the six high-rise office buildings.

❺ Donauturm★
☎ 263 35 72
Open every day 10am-11.30pm (in winter), 10am-midnight (in summer)
Entry charge.

The Danube Tower has a lift that takes just 35 seconds to reach the viewing platform of this huge building and costs around ATS70. From the top you'll have a panoramic view

If you can't spend a whole weekend without doing some sort of sport, then head for this small island in the Old Danube, which has become a paradise for the very active. Choose from tennis, volleyball, canoeing and sailing, or go to the Strandbad (beach pool) where you'll see some of the finest examples of post-war architecture.

❼ LA CRÊPERIE★★
An der oberen Alten Donau, 6
☎ 270 31 00

Open every day 10am-midnight.

This is a lovely restaurant on the banks of one of the branches of the Old Danube, where you can enjoy fish dishes on the terrace. It's a very romantic setting, particularly on a warm summer evening. If you prefer to be on a boat, take a picnic basket with some chilled champagne and serenade your loved one in the moonlight.

❹ Uno-City★
Wagramer Strasse, 3-5
☎ 260 60 33 28
Guided tours Mon.-Fri. 11am & 2pm.

The Vienna International Centre (aka Uno-City and VIC) has been the United Nations' no. 3 base since

of Donaupark, Vienna's second largest green space after the Prater, with an even more extensive view of the city from the two revolving restaurants just below.

❻ Gänsehaüfel★★
Moissigasse, 21.

Practicalities

HOTELS

In Austria there are five categories of hotel and four categories of pension, differentiated by a system of stars. In Vienna's 1st district there are over 30 luxury (5-star) and first class (4-star) hotels, but only a handful of 3-star ones. You'll find these in the districts beyond the Ringstrasse, but, as their comfort is only limited, it's probably wise to stay in one of the 4-star hotels and pensions in the first district. The pensions are often in office buildings or private houses, and are welcoming and pristine. Don't be too disappointed by the decor in some of the places — Viennese hotels are still trading on their nostalgic, fin-de-siècle appeal, and the furniture often looks a little shabby, the curtains and wall-hangings are always sombre and heavy, and the wallpaper often borders on kitsch.

Breakfast, on the other hand, is very substantial and if it's a buffet it will include cereal, muesli, eggs, bread rolls, cheeses, meat and yoghurt. Breakfast is normally included in the price of the room, and it will usually keep you going for most of the day.

PRICES

Generally speaking, there are two 'seasons' — summer/high season (*Sommersaison*) from 1 April to 31 October, and winter/low season (*Wintersaison*), from 1 November to 31 March. Winter prices tend to be lower, except for the two weeks over Christmas and New Year, for which there is often a surcharge or minimum stay requirement. If you decide to splash out and stay at one of the big luxury hotels on the Ringstrasse, check out their weekend packages, which also apply to some of the 4-star

hotels. Even with these special reductions, prices in the first district are quite high. A double room in a 4-star hotel will cost ATS2,300-2,900 a night. In a 4-star pension you'll be looking at ATS1,600-1,900 a night for a double room. In Austria you don't sleep between sheets, but under a quilt or duvet. King-sized beds are rare and are generally made up of twin beds pushed together.

BOOKING A ROOM

Vienna is a popular place to visit, particularly on New Year's Eve and during the ball season, when rooms in the city centre can be hard to find. You're strongly advised to book in advance, which you can do directly with the hotel or pension or through the Wien-Hotels company. This is the reservations department of the Vienna Tourist Office. You can contact them by phone on 43 (code for Austria) 12 11 140 or by fax on 43 12 11 14 445. They are open every day 8am-6pm (but closed on Sundays from November to March) and will give you a list of 'Hotels & Pensionen'. Alternatively, you can also access their website on the Internet (http://info.wien.at/) which offers an online booking service.

RESTAURANTS

The restaurant scene is really booming in Vienna. Until the 1970s the choice of restaurants and menus was not exceptional, but now the cuisine is much more varied, the standard of service has improved beyond measure and the city offers a culinary kaleidoscope, while still serving its traditional imperial dishes and regional specialities. The restaurants that serve genuine Viennese cooking are upholding the tradition of the *Beisln*, local pubs serving honest, local fare in unpretentious surroundings. You can go to a *Beisln* for a meal or for a beer or wine. You'll also find 'Balkan Grills', pizzerias, Creole and Indonesian restaurants and, in the shopping malls, fast food and self-service outlets, such as Akakiko (for sushi), Leiner (for Schnitzel) and Rosenberger (a self-service buffet). There are also some very trendy designer eating places, including Guess Club and Se'Stelle, launched by a team of fashionable architects and restaurant owners. Vienna has something to satisfy everyone's palate.

USEFUL TIPS

Viennese mealtimes, on the other hand, have remained much the same. Generally speaking, the locals eat relatively early — between 11.30am and 1pm for lunch and between 6.30 and 8pm for dinner. There are very few restaurants serving meals after 10pm. Drinking tap water in a restaurant is not an Austrian custom — they tend to drink sparkling mineral water, so you'll have to specify still water (*stilles Wasser*) if that's what you prefer. Beer is usually drunk by the *Krugerl* (half-litre/pint), but you can also have a *Seidl* (third of a litre/3/4 pint) or a *Pfiff* (eighth of a litre/1/4 pint) You can mix light (*hell*) and dark (*dunkel*) beer in a *Mischbier*, or have half beer, half lemonade, which is called a *Radler*. Draught beer is called *Bier vom Fass*. Wine is sometimes mixed with sparkling mineral water to make a *G'spritzt*. The locals tend to go to a café for their after-dinner coffee rather than having it in the restaurant.

PRICES

Lunch in a standard restaurant will cost about ATS250 and up to ATS400 in a smarter establishment, not including drinks. Wine is normally served by the glass as bottles can be prohibitively expensive. A meal in a *Kaffee-Konditorei* (in particular at Demel) can be pricey, but there are always the more reasonable set meals served by some restaurants. The price includes service, but it's customary to leave a 10% tip. Our selection features one star for restaurants where the main course on an á la carte menu costs under ATS165, two stars for a price range of ATS165-245, three stars for ATS245 and above, and four stars for top restaurants costing more than ATS340.

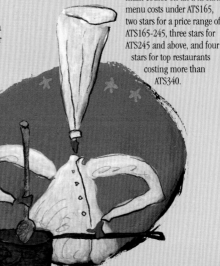

HOTELS

König von Ungarn★★★★

1, Schulerstrasse, 10
U-Bahn Stephansplatz
☎ 51 58 40
🅕 51 58 48
Double rooms ATS1,900-2,290.

This 18th-century building has 33 renovated rooms with double-glazing, rustic Styrian furniture and wonderfully soft mattresses. It has a charming covered courtyard where you can have breakfast and is in a perfect location, near the cathedral. It's a great little oasis and very popular, so remember to book well ahead. The restaurant is top-notch too.

Kaiserin Elisabeth★★★★

1, Weihburggasse, 3
U-Bahn Stephansplatz
☎ 51 52 60
🅕 515 267
Double rooms ATS1,900-2,450.

This prestigious hotel dating from 1809 was once the home of nobility, and of Wagner and Liszt. It hasn't lost its aristocratic air and charm, or its Biedermeier feel, although some might call the latter stuffy. The foyer has wonderful Persian carpets, and there are 53 rooms for fans of Empress Sissi.

Pertschy

1, Habsburgergasse, 5
U-Bahn Stephansplatz
☎ 53 44 90
🅕 534 49 49
Double rooms ATS1,280-1,480.

This pension is located in the courtyard of the Palais Cavriani, in the antiques distict. It has 47 rooms decorated with crystal lights in Rococo style looking onto the courtyard. Given its location, the prices are reasonable.

Nossek★★★

1, Graben, 7
U-Bahn Stephansplatz
☎ 533 70 41
🅕 535 36 46
Double rooms ATS1,050-1,600.

You couldn't be more central than in this large pension with 26 rooms on three floors of an old building on the Graben. Admittedly, the bathrooms are a little spartan, but it's highly recommended and you need to book in advance. It well deserves its three much-coveted stars.

Neuer Markt

1, Seilergasse, 9
U-Bahn Stephansplatz
☎ 512 23 16
🅕 513 91 05
Double rooms ATS1,100-1,500.

This is a very popular pension at the top of an imposing stairwell. It has 37 rooms, all with bath or

shower, and some with views over the Neuermarkt. It's a modest, unpretentious and charming place with reasonable prices given its location.

Römischer Kaiser★★★★

1, Annagasse, 16
U-Bahn Stephansplatz
☎ 512 77 51
🅕 512 77 51 13
Double rooms ATS1,990-3,190.

Housed in a Baroque palace dating from 1684, this hotel has 24 cosy bijou rooms, some of which are decorated in cream and brocade, others in gold or pink. It's ideally located only five minutes from the Opera, and the management will arrange tickets for the Boys' Choir or Spanish Riding School. All rooms have en suite facilities.

Mailberger Hof★★★★

1, Annagasse, 7
U-Bahn Stephansplatz
☎ 512 06 41
🅕 512 06 41 10
Double rooms ATS1,900-2,900.

This Baroque palace belonged for a long time to the Order of Malta and was transformed in 1976 into a family hotel with 40 luxurious rooms. Most look onto the interior courtyard, where you can have breakfast in summer. There's a weekend package of ATS3,000 for a double room, staying Friday and Saturday nights.

Aviano

1, Marco-D'Aviano-Gasse, 1
U-Bahn Stephansplatz
☎ 512 83 30
🅕 512 83 306
Double room ATS1,400.

This pension has 17 rooms decorated in flowery, pseudo-Viennese style. It's in an ideal location for night-owls looking for a drink at 2am, right next door to the Reiss Bar.

Sacher★★★★★

1, Philharmonikerstrasse, 4
U-Bahn Karlsplatz
☎ 51 4560
🅕 51 456 810.

Break open your piggy-bank and stay here, even if it's just for a night. It's Vienna's most celebrated hotel, founded in 1876 by Eduard Sacher, son of the inventor of the famous chocolate cake, the *Sachertorte*. Its 108 rooms are not huge but luxuriously furnished with wood-panelling and beautiful furniture, paintings and carpets, all kept in tip top condition by a team of craftsmen. It's popular with the Japanese, with conductors and tenors, for whom

the hotel is just an annex of the Opera, and with film directors. It used to be home to aristocratic playboys in the imperial days. A suite starts at ATS11,000 and can cost up to ATS39,000.

Freyung/ Synagogue

Palais Hotel★★★★

1, Rudolfsplatz, 11
U-Bahn Schottenring
☎ 533 13 53
🅕 533 13 53 70
e-mail kk.palais.hotel@kuk.at
Double rooms ATS2,020-2,350.

If you're looking for a hotel in a sleepy district with few tourists, then this is the place for you. Housed in a 19th-century building, once the town house of Franz Josef's mistress, Katharina Schratt, it's situated in the textile manufacturing quarter. It has 66 rooms that are all very clean and fully en suite. The hotel still has an imperial air about it.

Orient★

1, Tiefer Graben, 30
U-Bahn Herrengasse
☎ 533 73 07
🅕 535 03 40
Double rooms ATS1,200.

This fin-de-siècle hotel built in 1896 is close to the Gothic church of Maria am Gestade. Its decor is deliciously kitsch, and some of the scenes from 'The Third Man', with Orson Welles, were filmed here. The 26 rooms and suites are themed, some Oriental, others African or Viennese, and many people come here just for the decor. Staying at the Orient is an unusual experience.

Stubenviertel

Arenberg

1, Stubenring, 2
U-Bahn Stubentor
☎ 512 52 91
℉ 513 93 56
Double rooms ATS1,480-1,850.

Don't be put off by the outside – Arenberg is one of the most welcoming hotels in Vienna. There are only 25 rooms on two floors, but they're nicely decorated (though the wallpaper may not be to everyone's taste), and the tram stops just outside. Not only that, but the airport bus stop is just a five-minute walk away. A great little spot.

Spittelberg

Altstadt Vienna

7, Kirchengasse, 41
U-Bahn Volkstheater
☎ 526 33 99
℉ 523 49 01
Double rooms ATS1,280-1,880.

Just opposite the Baroque Ulrichskirche, and a seven-minute walk from the Ring and museum quarter, is this serene, elegant establishment with 25 rooms recently renovated by Herr Wiesenthal. The colours and fabrics were carefully chosen to create a harmonious atmosphere in the en suite rooms with high ceilings and wooden floors. The staff are very helpful.

Maria Theresia★★★★

7, Kirchberggasse, 6-8,
U-Bahn Volkstheater
☎ 521 23
℉ 21 23 70
Double rooms ATS2,020-2,350.

Located in the heart of Spittelberg, this is a modern hotel with 123 air-conditioned rooms housed in a building with an 18th-century façade. The decor is rather uniform, in shades of yellow with light wood and rattan furnishings, but there are fax and computer facilities for those who need to keep in touch with the office.

Mariahilf

Am Brillantengrund★★★

7, Bandgasse, 4
U-Bahn Zieglergasse
☎ 523 36 62
℉ 526 13 30
Double rooms ATS1,150-1,760.

Just a three-minute walk from the Imperial Furniture Collection, this little-known hotel with 32 rooms decorated in Biedermeier style is a really lovely place to stay. There's a bicycle stand for those of you who've decided to be energetic and discover Vienna's charms by bike.

Altwienerhof★★★

15, Herklotzgassse, 6
U-Bahn Gumpendorfer Strasse
☎ 892 60 00
℉ 892 60 008
Double rooms ATS980-2,000.

This hotel has a renowned restaurant, and its 22 rooms are just as delightful, luxuriously decorated with lace, marble and velvet. You can have breakfast outside in the summer or in the covered courtyard in less clement weather. A good place to stay.

Housed in a 19th-century bourgeois building and situated close to the Concert Hall, this hotel has charming rooms decorated in Biedermeier or Jugendstil style (ask for a room at the back). The atmosphere is calm and peaceful, and the clientèle smart rather than trendy.

Ring

Ana Grand Hotel★★★★★

1, Kärtner Ring, 9
U-Bahn Karlsplatz
☎ 51 58 00
📠 515 13 13
E-mail: Sales@ana.grand.com
Double rooms ATS4,500.

This prestigious establishment is owned by All Nippon Airways and well deserves its five stars. It offers 205 faultlessly luxurious rooms at what can only be described as 'imperial' prices. You might like to take advantage of the 'Vienna shopping' package at ATS3,190 or the weekend deal of ATS3,540 (both prices per night for a double room).

Bristol★★★★

1, Kärntner Ring 1
U-Bahn Karlsplatz
☎ 515 16 0
📠 515 16 550
Double rooms from 3,900ATS.

Since 1892, this legendary hotel from the Austro-Hungarian Empire has been a favourite place to stay for singers and virtuosos. The hotel is renowned for its hospitality, its wonderful view of the Opera and its 11 divine suites and 114 rooms, all decorated in opulent style with

antiques and wonderfully crafted furniture. Come here for a weekend of comfort, style and charm. The elegant Korso bei der Oper restaurant is one of Vienna's finest and a visual feast, too, with its marble columns.

Am Schubertring★★★★

1, Schubertring, 1
U-Bahn Stadtpark
☎ 71 70 20
📠 713 99 66
Double rooms from ATS1,550 (low season).

Naschmarkt

Schneider★★★★

6, Getreidemarkt, 5
U-Bahn Karlsplatz
☎ 58 83 80
📠 588 38 212
Double rooms ATS154.

Situated next to the Secession building and Academy of Fine Arts, this hotel has a slightly forbidding exterior which conceals, however, an unpretentious establishment with spacious and comfortable rooms. There are also studio rooms with kitchenettes for those who want to try out recipes using the products they buy from the Naschmarkt.

RESTAURANTS

Stephansdom

Cantinetta Antinori★★

1, Jasomir-Gott-Strasse, 3/5,
U-Bahn Stephansplatz
☎ 533 77 22

Open every day 11.30am-3pm, 6pm-midnight.

This is unquestionably the best Italian restaurant in Vienna. The dining room looks like the loggia of a Medici villa, and everyone comes here to enjoy the chef's creations, perfected during his experience both in Florence and Zurich. His guinea-fowl with fresh rosemary (ATS185) is a delight, and the wine and olive oil come straight from the Tuscan hills.

Wrenkh★★

1, Bauernmarket, 10
U-Bahn Stephansplatz
☎ 533 15 26
Open Mon.-Sat. 11am-11pm.

Wrenkh is a very popular with trendy vegetarians, who enjoy the designer decor in wood by Eichinger and Knechtl, and the risotto and tofu dishes. The food is elegantly served but quite pricey. An evening meal costs from ATS185, but it's a fashionable place to dine.

Carmina Burana★

1, Singerstrasse, 22
U-Bahn Stephansplatz
☎ 512 34 59
Open Mon.-Sat.
11am-midnight.

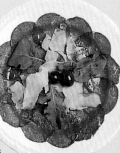

Fresh pasta with salmon (ATS135), and *rigatoni* with tomato, basil and mozarella make this a compulsory stop when you're doing your shopping in this district. It's a tiny restaurant with only six tables and three bar stools at the counter. Try the *prosecco,* and gaze at the painted nudes on the walls.

Weibel's Bistro★★

1, Rienergasse, 1-3
U-Bahn Stephansplatz
☎ 513 31 10
Open Mon.-Fri. 10am-12.30am, Sat. 5pm-12.30am.

Hans Weibel has a wonderful wine cellar and already owns two other properties in Vienna's 1st district (Kumpfgasse, 2, and Wollzeile, 5). His newest establishment is just as successful and offers tasty dishes that are refreshingly light and have an Italian/ French/ Viennese slant. A house speciality is medallions of pork fillet coated in sage and served with green beans and polenta, a culinary triumph which will set you back ATS195.

Karntnerstrasse

A Tavola★

1, Weihburggasse, 3-5
U-Bahn Stephansplatz
☎ 512 79 55
Open Mon.-Sat. noon-3pm, 6pm-midnight.

This is a trendy designer Italian *osteria*, whose cave-like interior has been sponged with orange and white. A favourite spot for local business people, it can get rather loud and busy at peak times. Try the pasta dishes (ATS95-115), the *involtini di manzo,* or some of the inventive Tuscan cuisine. The service is efficient, with the waiters dressed in large red aprons.

Drei Husaren★★★★

1, Weihburggasse, 4
U-Bahn Stephansplatz
☎ 512 10 92 0
Open every day noon-3pm, 6pm-1am.

'The Three Hussars' is one of Vienna's top restaurants. It has an elegant interior with chandeliers, crystal and cut glass on the table, and a piano on which Chopin is played in the evening. The service

...is very smooth and courteous, and it will cost you ATS800 a head, not including wine. Closed mid-July to mid-August.

Barbaro's★★

1, Kärntner Strasse, 19
U-Bahn Stephansplatz
☎ 513 17 12 25
Open every day 11.30am-4pm, 6pm-midnight.

You can't miss Barbaro's. It's on the seventh and last floor of the department store, Steffl, and Martin Stanek serves delicious calamari, wild boar paté with balsamic vinegar (ATS155) and pizzas for those in a hurry to get back to their shopping. The seats are a little uncomfortable, but the view over the city rooftops is really magnificent.

Freyung/Synagogue

Kupferdachl★★

1, Schottengasse, 7
U-Bahn Schottentor
☎ 533 93 81 14
Open Mon.-Fri. noon-3pm, 6pm-midnight,
Sat. 6pm-midnight.

This restaurant, renowned for its wine list and lavish St Silvester dinners (ATS895), has a very opulent dining room with subtle lighting, where all the great Viennese classic dishes are served. You'll find Tafelspitz, Lungenbraten, Apfelstrudel and the rest. This is the place for those with large appetites keen to try traditional fare.

Hansen★★

1, Wipplingerstrasse, 34
U-Bahn Schottentor
☎ 532 05 42
Open Mon.-Fri. 9am-9pm, Sat. 9am-5pm.

You'd never have guessed that one of Vienna's best eating places is housed in the basement of the Stock Exchange (*Börse*). The chef, Christian Voithofer, creates innovative dishes using seasonal produce, including dates, pistachio nuts and marzipan. It's a refreshing surprise and dishes cost from ATS85-135. Try the salmon fillet in red wine and chestnuts – it's really delicious.

Divine★★

1, Neutorgasse
U-Bahn Schottenring
☎ 532 10 78
Open every day 11am-2pm (weekends until 4pm).

Meat lovers will be able to gorge on huge steaks here for ATS195, washed down with a bottle of Blauer Zweigelt, whilst listening to funk and soul music. The service is very friendly and the interior is rather loft-like, with exposed pipes, red curtains and black linoleum (the owner is a former croupier). You need to book in advance for the weekend, as it gets very busy. It's a fun place to come.

Ofenloch★

1, Kurrentgasse, 8
U-Bahn Herrengasse
☎ 533 88 44
Open every day 11.30am-10.45pm.

This is a quaint rustic *Beisl* (local pub) founded in 1704 serving traditional Viennese dishes with fresh mushrooms and a Czech flavour for an increasingly cosmopolitan clientèle. Lunch costs around ATS165.

Salzamt★

1, Ruprechtsplatz, 1
U-Bahn Schwedenplatz
☎ 533 53 32
Open every day 5pm-4am, kitchen until 12.30am.

Salzamt is a hard core 'Bermuda Triangle' establishment (see p. 41). The minimalist decor is by Hermann Czech, the clientèle is

very yuppy, young and fashionable and the menu has a strong Italian influence to it. Enjoy a dish of carpaccio and parmesan (ATS110) or the Moravian *Topfen* (quark) with poppy seeds and plum jam. This is a fun place to have a meal before heading out to the district's many bars.

Stubenviertel

Plachutta★★★

1, Wollzeile, 38
U-Bahn Stubentor
☎ 512 15 77
Open every day 11.30am-2.30pm, 6-10.30pm.

The chances of your eating *Schnitzel* and *Tafelspitz* during your stay in Vienna are very high so you should know where to get the best. This famous restaurant is pricey (ATS255 for loin of beef) but the dishes are fabulous and the service faultless. You need to book well ahead.

Hofburg

Grotta Azzura★★★

1, Babenbergerstrasse, 5
U-Bahn Babenbergerstrasse
☎ 586 10 44 0
Open every day noon-3pm, 6pm-midnight.

This is another temple of gastronomy located just behind the Akademie der bildenden Künste. Walter Hofwagner prepares wonderful classic dishes from Northern Italy, and his salmon trout from Lake Garda is unbelievable (ATS195). The decor is slightly overdone, with Murano glass lamps and mosaics from Capri, but it's certainly worth a visit.

Spittelberg/Rathaus

Witwe Bolte★

7, Gutenberggasse, 13
U-Bahn Volkstheater
☎ 523 14 50
Open Mon.-Sat. 11.30am-2.30pm, 5.30-11.30pm.

More and more tourists come to this *Wiener Beisl* to taste the calf's liver with juniper berries, roast pork with potato croquettes and other house specialities (*Schmankerl*). It's traditional cooking and not very low-fat! Dishes cost around ATS160 and there's a lovely garden in summer.

Alte Backstube★★

8, Lange Gasse, 34
U-Bahn Rathaus
☎ 406 11 01
Open Mon.-Sat. 11am-midnight (Sun. from 5pm)

Between 1697 and 1963 this ornate building was used as a bakery. Brigitte Schwarzmann now serves imaginative Austrian food that needs to be taken seriously. For those not especially

keen on loin of beef (ATS195), and for those who don't like meat in general *(fia der de fleischlos glicklich san)*, there are vegetarian dishes. Note that the restaurant closes from mid-July to mid-August.

Ring

Unkai★★★

1, Kärntner Ring, 9
U-Bahn Karlsplatz
☎ 515 80 91 10
Open Mon. 6-10.45pm,
Tue.-Sun. noon-2.30pm,
6-10.45pm

This Japanese restaurant is on the seventh floor of the Ana Grand Hotel. You'll be dining at ground level, sitting on a *tatami*, or round the grill, in an elegant room decorated with sand-coloured and lacquered black furnishings, under the watchful eye of Yoshinobu Nozawa. At lunchtime on Saturdays and Sundays you can enjoy a 'sushi brunch' for ATS390 per person, including green tea and *miso* soup. It is a delightful experience.

Alsergrund

Stomach★★

9, Seegasse, 26
U-Bahn Roßauer Lande
☎ 310 20 99
Open Wed.-Sat. 6-11.30pm,
Sun. noon-11.30pm.

Just a stone's throw from the Palais Lichtenstein, you can enjoy large helpings at great prices in the lovely garden or in the rustic Styrian setting. All the produce is fresh and natural and melts in the mouth. Worth dropping in.

Heurigen

Wieninger★

21, Stammersdorfer
Strasse, 78
Tram 31 to terminus
☎ 292 41 06
Open Wed.-Fri. 3pm-
midnight, Sat.-Sun. 1pm-
midnight.

Fritz Wieninger is a rising star of Austrian wine growing, whose brother, Leo, opens his wonderful Heuriger in the Stammersdorf district from March until mid-December. Here you can taste the most recent vintage and enjoy a green bean salad and black

sausage with a glass of chilled Chardonnay.

Schreiberhaus★

19, Rathstrasse, 54
Bus 35a from U-Bahn
Nussdorfer Strasse
☎ 440 38 44 or 440 38 39
Open every day 11am-1am.

This *Heuriger* is in Neustift am Walde and is a good place to quench your thirst after a long walk in the Vienna Woods. Decorated in Laura Ashley style, it serves pleasant chilled wines.

Göbel★

21, Hagenbrunner Strasse, 151
☎ 294 84 20
Bus 228
Open 11am-11pm Apr.-Oct.
(from 1st Sat.-3rd Sun. in
month)

If it's a sunny day, head out to the lovely Bisamberg vines, where winemaker Hans Peter Gobel has a delightful country tavern (*Buschenschank*). He serves great red wines, accompanied by salads, wild boar and vegetables.

CAFÉS AND TEAROOMS

Hawelka

1, Dorotheergasse, 6
☎ 512 82 30
U-Bahn Stephansplatz
Open Mon., Wed.- Sat. 8am-2am, Sun. 4pm-2am.

The legendary Hawelka café is very popular, so you may have to fight for a table. It's a bohemian place frequented by intellectuals and literati, as well as tourists reading the international papers. It's quite dark and smoky and has a limited choice of teas and pastries, but has a really great atmosphere.

Kleines Café

1, Frankziskanerplatz, 3
U-Bahn Stephansplatz
Open Mon-Sat. 10am-2am, Sun. 1pm-2am.

This is one of Vienna's smallest cafés, with only six tables in a vaulted room, but it's very cosy. Designed by the Viennese architect Hermann Czech in the 1970s, it was one of the first *Kaffeebäuser* to be mod ernised. It serves delicious omelettes, sausages and goat's cheese with olive sandwiches served on wooden platters. Worth a visit.

Sluka

1, Rathausplatz, 8
U-Bahn Rathaus
☎ 405 71 72
Open Mon.-Fri. 8am-7pm, Sat. 8am-5.30pm.

If your happiness is greatly increased by the sight of a cake drenched in Chantilly cream, this *Kaffee-Konditorei* is the place for you. The all-white cake shop, decorated with mirrors and chandeliers, is under the arches near the Town Hall. It's a haven of tranquillity as well as a gourmet's paradise.

Sperl

6, Gumpendorfer Strasse, 11
U-Bahn Karlsplatz/Babenbergerstrasse
☎ 586 41 58
Open Mon.-Sat. 7am-11pm, Sun. 3-11pm.

This was voted best café in Vienna in 1998 and is a renowned *Kaffeehaus*. It's L-shaped and slightly shabby despite having been only recently renovated. Sperl was the former headquarters of the Austrian Secessionist movement, whose followers would meet to discuss art and architecture and to doodle on the tablecloths, its clientèle today consists mainly of impoverished but talented students, billiard players and journalists.

Prückl

1, Stubenring, 24
U-Bahn Stubentor
☎ 512 61 15
Open every day 9am-10pm.

The Prückl is very close to the MAK and the Stadtpark. If you're a fan of the 1950s look, this is the place for you. It's a bright, airy and relaxed café, where you can play bridge and meet friendly folk. It has large bay windows, a terrace and a resident pianist in the evening to entertain you.

Landtmann

1, Dr Karl-Lueger-Ring, 4
U-Bahn Herrengasse
tel 533 91 28
Open every day 8am-midnight.

Landtmann is one of Vienna's most upmarket and elegant *Kaffeehäuser* and Freud's favourite. It's ideally situated

between the university, the theatre and the Town Hall. Its clientèle is therefore quite varied, with actors, politicians and students all enjoying their coffee in a turn-of-the-century decor of mirrors and wood. You can eat on the terrace in the summer and delight in the vanilla-flavoured *Buchtel* at any time of year. There's also a cellar for fringe theatre.

Lehmann

1, Graben, 12
U-Bahn Stephansplatz
☎ **512 18 18**
Open Mon.-Sat. 8.30am-7pm.

You may find it hard to get a table at this very popular and elegant *Konditorei* (patisserie).

The sandwiches are delicious, and there's a wide selection of pastries including *Dobos* and *Esterházy,* for those of you who love chocolate, cream and icing. Worth a visit just for these.

where there are more tourists than locals. The decor is red and gold, with imperial portraits on the walls, and cakes made by head pastry chef Friedrich Pflieger. The famous cake, the *Sachertorte,* is served with whipped cream, and the recipe is still based on the original.

Tichy

10, Reumannplatz, 13
U-Bahn Reumannplatz
☎ **604 44 46**
Open 10am-11pm.10h-23h.

At the end of the U1 line, the most famous of Austria's ice-cream parlours has over fifteen flavours for your delectation, including *Eis-Marillenknödel* (apricot) and *Erdbeer* (strawberry).

Zanoni

1, Lugeck, 7
U-Bahn Stephansplatz
☎ **512 79 79**
Open every day 10am-11pm.

The king of Italian ice-cream in Vienna is Luciano Zanoni. For ATS17 you can have a delicious bilberry sorbet, or a *gelato.*

Sacher

I, Philharmonikerstrasse, 4
U-Bahn Karlsplatz
☎ **512 14 87**
Open every day 7.30-11.30pm.

Put on your best outfit and enjoy yourself at this renowned café,

Practicalities

The City is the historical and political centre of Vienna, but it's also the hub of tourist and shopping activity. Kärntnerstrasse is excellent for browsing and high-class window-shopping, as are Graben and Kohlmarkt. Close to the Hofburg you'll find all the former imperial suppliers, the silversmiths, antique shops and fashion houses, whose prices are sometimes as stunning as their products. The streets of Neubau, north of Mariahilferstrasse, are worth a look, too.

THE BEST PLACES TO SHOP

In the surrounding districts, in particular Hoher Markt, Am Hof, Naglergasse, Rotenturmstrasse and Singerstrasse, the shops are considerably less ostentatious, noticeably more original and fractionally less expensive. Not too far away is Mariahilferstrasse, Vienna's main shopping street, where the shop assistants tend to be less surly than their City colleagues. It's a godsend for those with tired feet, as it's easy to get to by tram, bus or metro. However, it's best avoided on a Saturday in December, when hordes of shoppers descend on the street. You'll find Virgin Megastore, but it's mostly full of Austrian stores, including Gerngross. The SCS (*Shopping City Süd*) in Vösendorf gets very busy, too, and is considered to be the mecca of Austrian shopping. It's the largest shopping complex in the country and is south of the city limits. A tram runs from the shop opposite the Staatsoper to Baden.

OPENING TIMES

The shops in the 1st district, in the triangle formed by the Cathedral, Opera and Kohlmarkt, are usually open Monday to Friday 9am to 6pm. On Saturdays they tend to close at 5pm, but shops in other areas often close on Saturday afternoons, too, except on the first Saturday of the month. A few shops shut for an hour or so at lunch, and only some of the department stores on the Mariahilferstrasse stay open until 7pm on weekdays and 6pm at weekends. Food shops have a different set of opening hours entirely, opening their doors from between 7am and 8am until between 7pm or 8pm, except on Saturday when they may close either at 1pm or 5pm. Florists, tobacconists, pharmacies and grocers at the airport situated in the Westbahnhof and Südbahnhof are open Monday to Sunday 7am to 10.30pm.

BEST METHODS OF PAYMENT

The majority of the shops in the 1st district and in Mariahilf take credit cards, in particular Visa, Eurocard, Diner's Club and American Express. Just check the stickers in the window or on the door before you commit yourself to buying. Eurocheques are accepted everywhere, but you have to pay a commission charge. The best thing is to withdraw cash at a *bankomat* (cash machine). If you lose your cards, call the following numbers:

☎ 71 11 10 for Visa
☎ 71 70 10 for Eurocard
☎ 50 13 50 for Diner's Club
☎ 515 110 or ☎ 660 68 40 for American Express

FINDING YOUR WAY AROUND

In the Shopping and Nightlife sections, you'll find a reference after each address to its position on the map on p. 80-81.

TAX REFUNDS

If you live outside the EU and have bought a pretty vase or a genuine Loden cape to the value of ATS1000 or more from a shop calling itself 'duty-free', you can be reimbursed for the Austrian VAT (*Mehrwertsteuer*), charged at 13%. Ask the sales person to complete a U34 or tax exemption form and present this at customs when you leave Austria. The 13% tax should then be refunded to you in cash.

SHIPPING GOODS HOME

Most furniture, carpet or interior design shops can arrange for your larger purchases to be sent to your home by a reliable transport company. Ask them for a quote based on size and distance, including insurance. Alternatively, try: Horst Auer Internationale Spedition, 1 Dominikanerbastel, 20 ☎ 51 31 62 90.

LOST PROPERTY

If you're unfortunate enough to lose something of value, call the Fundamt on ☎ 313 44 92 14.

CUSTOMS REGULATIONS

As a signatory of the Schengen agreement, Austria does not make systematic customs checks at its border on nationals of EU countries. Residents of the US can take

SALES AND BARGAINS

Except for special offers (*Sonderangebote)* and the January and July sales, with their reductions on clothes, household items and electrical goods, you won't find too many bargains in Vienna. Prices on items are fixed and not open to negotiation. You'll only be able to enjoy a spot of haggling at the flea market (Flohmarkt, see p. 115) and at the smaller Saturday markets (Am Hof, Freyung, and Schwedenplatz). Your Vienna Card (see p. 37) entitles you to reductions of around 10% in selected shops (Österreichische Werkstätten, Nowotny, Backhausen and in some Bakalowits) and department stores (Steffl, Gerngross, and the Ringstrassen-Galerien).

up to 200 cigarettes or 200gm/ 7oz of tobacco and 1 litre of wine or spirits. Canadians can take 250 cigarettes or 200gm/7oz of tobacco, 50 cigars, 1.5 litres of wine or 1.4 litres of spirits. Australian citizens must limit themselves to 200 cigarettes or 250gm/9oz of tobacco and 1 litre of wine or spirits. New Zealanders are allowed 200 cigarettes or 250gm/9oz of tobacco, 4.5 litres of beer or wine and 1 litre of spirits. Customs officials are very strict about importing any goods that are imitations. They are immediately confiscated along with the vehicle in which they are transported. The offender is then heavily fined. Amounts vary but can be up to double the value of the authentic items.

EMBASSIES

Australia
4, Mattiellistrasse, 2-4
☎ 512 85 80

Canada
1, Laurenzerberg, 2
☎ 531 38 30 00

UK
3, Jauresgasse, 12
☎ 716 13

USA
9, Bolzmanngasse, 16
☎ 313 39

WOMEN'S FASHION

Fashion in Vienna may at first seem rather classic and unadventurous, and it's true that traditional Austrian dress (*Tracht*) is still worn, with women in *Dirndls* (dresses with full skirts and lace blouses) and men in *Walker* (green cloth jackets) or *Loden* (capes). However, this is changing. A new generation of young designers is at work, inventing new and much more exciting styles.

KNITWEAR

Atlas

Bäckerstrasse, 3 (C2)
U-Bahn Stephansplatz
☎ 512 98 50
Open Mon.-Fri. 11am-6pm, Sat. 11am-5pm.

This is a shop with a wood and metal decor, where you can buy thick cashmere jumpers (ATS1,880), that will make you look like Little Red Riding Hood. Don't miss the lovely pullovers by Katharine Hamnett (ATS3,550) and Massimo Rebecchi (ATS1,650).

Sebastian

Jasomirgottstrasse, 2 (B2)
U-Bahn Stephansplatz
☎ 533 61 53
Open Mon.-Fri. 11am-6pm, Sat. 11am-5pm.

Sebastian, Atlas's smaller sister store has comfy (*kuschelig*) fashions for sale. Some fabrics are so pale and soft to look at and touch that they look more like marshmallows than jumpers. If you feel the cold, try a pullover made locally in 100% natural fabrics (ATS1,000) – you won't want to take it off. For a more unstructured look, try a Nicole Farhi top in natural wool (ATS3,250).

Haider-Petkov

Wollzeile, 6 (C2)
U-Bahn Stephansplatz
☎ 512 38 23
Open Mon.-Fri. 11am-6pm, Sat. 11am-5pm.

Since the baton of the Haider-Petkov name was handed over, Suzanne, the designer, and Manfred, the technical expert, haven't looked back. Their knitwear in mohair, Lurex or polyester is very sophisticated and fluid in style, with very subtle use of transparency One of their more humorous designs uses browns and blues to make a jumper resembling a Venetian blind (ATS4,900). You can buy some of their creations at lower prices on the first floor of the Outletcenter, Mariahilferstrasse, 101-108, open Mon-Fri. 2-7pm, ☎ 597 62 74.

AUSTRIAN FASHION DESIGNERS

Modus vivendi

**Schadekgasse, 4 (not on map)
U-Bahn Neubaugasse
☎ 587 28 23
Open Mon.-Fri. 10am-7pm, Sat. noon-4pm.**

Monika Hacher has opened her shop in an area not known for being at the height of fashion. She only has a sofa, swing mirror and a few dummies in an intentionally modest and unassuming setting, in which she

sells her own range of perfumes alongside her classic clothes. There are pretty shirts with green, cream, violet or brown collars (ATS980), and jumpers in 100% merino wool (ATS1,900) in a rainbow of colours. It's a lovely shop, with friendly staff and good prices. When the new collection comes out, the Modus vivendi team serves pumpkin soup and punch.

Helmut Lang

**Seilergasse, 6 (C3)
U-Bahn Stephansplatz
☎ 513 25 88
Open Mon.-Fri. 10am-6.30pm, Sat. 10am-5pm.**

The famous Austrian, Helmut Lang, teaches fashion at the School of Applied Arts in Vienna, and the shop at this address is much less impersonal than the one in the Printemps department store in Paris. His perfectly fitted fuchsia red sleeveless dresses cost ATS7,500, and his fluffy coats are a cool ATS11,000ATS. It's the place to come if you need a new pair of jeans spattered with paint Jackson Pollock style. A must for every wardrobe.

Doris Ainedter

**Jasomirgottstrasse, 5 (B2)
U-Bahn Stephansplatz
☎ 532 03 69
Open Mon.-Sat. 10am-6.30pm.**

Doris Ainedter has come up with two innovative collections aimed at women who want to be able to go out straight from work without having to go home to change. 'Business' and 'Top Fashionable' have replaced the neat little suit with cocktail dresses (ATS11,890) and classic black jackets (ATS4,790). These can be worn with equal style in a restaurant or a conference room. Her clothes are comfortable, practical, stylish and flexible – just what a busy woman needs in her wardrobe. Crafty shoppers will head for the Outlet-store at Marc-Aurel Strasse, 4, ☎ 533 58 93, where some of her clothes are sold at reduced prices.

Passage

Wipplingerstrasse, 7 (A1)
U-Bahn Stephansplatz
☎ 533 65 88
**Open Mon.-Fri. 10am-
1.30pm, 3-6pm, Sat. 10am-
1pm.**

This tiny shop has a delightful
treasure trove of clothes created by
several relatively unknown
designers, including Nomi's lovely
silk waistcoats costing ATS3,500,

Rachel Deutsch's beautiful hand-
painted scarves and Eva Blut's
attractive bags at ATS1,990, not
forgetting Semi Dei's 'Stretch'
velvet one-piece suits from
ATS6,950. Great things sometime
come in small packages as
Passage demonstrates.

STREETWEAR
AND AVANT-GARDE

Song

Landskrongasse, 2 (C2)
U-Bahn Stephansplatz
☎ 532 28 58
**Open Mon.-Fri. 10am-
6.30pm, Sat. 10am-6pm.**

The young Japanese owner of Song
has some carefully selected and
really stunning creations on show,
including Martin Margiella clothes
and designs by Ter & Bantine of
Milan. Grey flannel coats at
ATS13,500 and Ozzy Oswald's silver
and amethyst rings at ATS4,500 are
among the many delights you'll
find here. Keep in touch with the
latest fashions on their website,
www.song.at. Do a virtual tour of
next season's highlights.

In Wear

**Mariahilfer Strasse, 55 (not
on map)**
U-Bahn Neubaugasse
☎ 585 54 81
**Open Mon.-Fri.
9.30am-7pm, Sat.
9.30am-5pm.**

This shop has ready-
to-wear clothes from
Scandinavia for the
young and cool of
Vienna. The city is
one of only a few in
Europe – among
them Copenhagen,
Stockholm, Helsinki
and Rotterdam – to
have In Wear outlets
as yet. The staff
are extremely
friendly, the prices
reasonable
and the clothes
really gorgeous.
Try a *rollis*
(a polo-neck
jumper at
ATS298) or a
pair of 'Stretch'
trousers (ATS498),
or be a bit more
adventurous and
buy a 'Lolita' top
for ATS798.

Front Line

**Mariahilfer Strasse, 77-
79 (not on map)**
**U-Bahn
Neubaugasse**
☎ 586
30 68
**Open
Mon.-
Fri.,
10am-
7pm,
Sat.
10am-5pm.**

If you're looking
for the Front Line
the punks used to
buy all their
clothes from in the
70s, you're in the
wrong place. That
Front Line is near the
Lobkowitz Bridge, best
reached by U-Bahn
Meidling. This Front
Line is in the Generali-
Center and Reinhard
Maier has an eclectic
collection of street wear.
Don't miss the creations
of Tünde Kemenesi,
a young Hungarian
designer whose velvet
and taffeta waistcoats are
very theatrical.

INTERNATIONAL DESIGNERS

Knize

Graben 13 (B2)
U-Bahn Stephansplatz
☎ **512 21 190**
Open Mon.-Fri. 9.30am-6pm, Sat. 10am-5pm.

The decor of this very prestigious shop has been given a new, young look, but the clothes on sale are still just as sophisticated and the prices just as high (ATS25,000 for a lovely Italian blazer in 100% cashmere, for example). However, there are some waistcoats and jackets at more reasonable prices, which you can match with a bag by the Viennese designer, La Obra.

Fürnkranz

Karntnerstrasse 39 (B3)
U-Bahn Stephansplatz
☎ **488 440**
Open Mon.-Fri. 9.30am-6.30pm, Sat. 10am-6pm.

Fürnkranz has just celebrated its thirtieth birthday, and here you can find the major designers, such as Lacroix, Mugler, Rena Lange, Kiton and Joop. The shop, which is on three floors, features a flurry of shop assistants and lovely collections of classic and tasteful clothes. The prices are in line with other major European cities.

FUR MAKES A COMEBACK

Vienna used to be renowned for its wonderful fur coats, and there are still a few sought-after furriers (*Pelzhäuser*) making ribbed mink cuffs, fox muffs, marmot and silk jackets and 'new look' Russian-style fur hats. There are several furriers in Vienna, but here are just two that you can try:
Weinstein (1010, Hoher Markt, 9 (C2), ☎ 533 34 51)
Busta (1010, Schulerstrasse, 22 (C2), ☎ 512 28 46).
Both shops will also carry out repairs for you.

Amicis

Parkring, 12 (C/D3)
U-Bahn Stubentor
☎ **513 26 36**
Open Mon.-Fri. 10.30am-6.30pm, Sat. 10am-6pm.

Just a stone's throw from the Hilton, Marriot and Intercontinental hotels, this large space designed by the architect Redo Maggi houses a selection of Italian labels, including Allegri, Cerruti, Fusco and Dolce & Gabbana. There's also a dangerous collection of accessories – if you're feeling extravagant, beware. This is a VIP shopping experience.

MEN'S FASHION

Whether you're looking for something smart to wear to the office or something more relaxed and fun for an evening at a café or club, then Vienna won't disappoint you. Head for the 1st district for lovely lambswool jumpers or charcoal grey suits – you won't be besieged by the latest fashion crazes. The Mariahilf-Neubau district is the place to go for more informal attire, high on comfort and style but low on price. If you've nothing to wear to go dancing in one of Vienna's nightclubs, you'll be sure to find something here.

Herr Knize is an exclusive Viennese tailor. In the splendid workshop on the first floor of the narrow shop (designed in 1913 by Adolf Loos) the flannel or Prince of Wales check fabric is cut out and the elegant three-piece suits are put together and impeccably finished, usually in three weeks. They're as smart and perfectly made as anything you're likely to see in a gentleman's club. Try to resist the temptation to buy one of the pure cashmere scarves (ATS2,990) – it's not easy.

Harry & Sons

Am Hof, 5 (B2)
U-Bahn Herrengasse
☎ 533 36 66
Open Mon.-Fri. 10am-6.30pm, Sat. 10am-5pm.

This Italian shirt-maker already has 60 shops in Italy and has just opened its first two stores outside the country – in Thessalonica and here in Vienna. You won't find any eccentric or exotic designs, but there's a huge selection of stripes and checks for work or for play, ranging in price from ATS1,000-1,200. There's a little extra touch on the cuffs, where the buttons feature Botticelli's Venus wearing sunglasses.

Knize

Graben, 13 (B2
U-Bahn Stephansplatz
☎ 512 21 190
Open Mon.-Fri. 9.30am-6pm, Sat. 10am-5pm.

The Misfit

Gumpendorfer Strasse, 36
(not on map)
U-Bahn Kettenbrückengasse
☎ 586 16 99

Open Mon.-Fri. 11am-6pm,
Sat. 11am-2pm.

This is one of the few shops in Vienna where you're certain to find the trendy item that will get you noticed. Roland Zimmermann is very friendly and has his finger on the fashion pulse. Some of his stock is from abroad, such as the 'Books' jackets with hoods and the jumpers coated in rubber (ATS1,400) from Holland. The majority of the clothes are from his personal collection, eagerly snapped up by the lucky trendy locals. His viscose and polyamide suits cost ATS5,400 and have a fluid and relaxed line, perfect for city living. He can also make you a more exotic outfit for a special

occasion. This usually takes two to three weeks and is worth waiting for.

Kent

Rotenturmstrasse, 13 (C2)
U-Bahn Stephansplatz
☎ 533 73 62
Open Mon.-Fri. 9.30am-6.30pm, Sat. 9.30am-5pm.

Here's the place to come if you'd like to buy British. Kent specialises in knitwear and has lovely lambswool jumpers from Burlington, Castri sweaters from ATS1,490 and lisle socks. You can buy classic trousers, duffle coats and bomber jackets together with more casual holiday wear.

IT'S ALL IN THE COLLAR

The shirt plays a central role in a man's wardrobe, and the collar is a key element of its design. Today there are many shapes to choose from, including round, flat, Mao-style and 'Wall Street'. You should make your choice according to the shape of your face. Those with rather round faces should choose Italian collars with short and wide points, whereas the button-down collar is better suited to those with smaller faces and longer necks.

Schwanda

Backerstrasse, 17 (C2)
U-Bahn Stephansplatz
☎ 512 53 20
Open Mon.-Fri. 10am-6.30pm, Sat. 10am-5pm.

Schwanda is a real find for those who like to spend their time

outdoors and for locals who enjoy the Austrian Alps. If you feel like climbing a few mountains or just taking a walk in the Vienna Woods, pop into this shop for all the necessary gear in the latest hi-tech fabrics. We suggest the multi-pocketed survival jacket at around ATS2,500, which is suitable for most activities and an essential in every active person's wardrobe.

Dantendorfer

Weihburggasse, 9 (C3)
U-Bahn Stephansplatz
☎ 512 59 65
Open Mon.-Fri. 9.30am-6pm, Sat. 9.30am-5pm.

Most of the shirts at Dantendorfer tend to be rather classic and timeless, but there's no limit to the choice of colours, patterns and fabrics. They cost around ATS1,000, and you'll also find a selection of more adventurous labels including Ralph Lauren and Etro.

Ferman

Kramergasse, 9 (C2)
U-Bahn Stephansplatz
☎ 533 34 26
Open Mon.-Fri. 10am-6pm, Sat. 10am-5pm.

Ferdinand Mandel has a range of classic and tasteful shirts starting at ATS698, as well as silk, linen and cotton scarves and ties with floral or paisley patterns (ATS498). It's a good place to shop, so try to pop in.

HATS, BAGS, JEWELLERY AND OTHER ACCESSORIES

While you're in Vienna, why not treat yourself to that little frivolous but very meaningful something you've been looking for. Vienna has wonderful accessories shops where the products may be a bit expensive but are often handcrafted, with excellent finishing touches. Here are a few suggestions on the best places to go to find beautiful and imaginative gifts (for yourself).

Pitti

**Mariahilfer Strasse, 31
(not on map)
U-Bahn Babenbergerstrasse
☎ 586 34 83
Open Mon.-Fri. 10am-6pm,
Sat. 10am-5pm.**

This shop invites you to pack your bags and travel. It has a wonderful array of light suitcases, and soft and semi-rigid bags by Coccinelle, Mandarina Duck and DKNY. There are also some very nice Italian brands, in particular a green Furla *borsa* at ATS1,980.

R. Horn

**Braunerstrasse, 7 (B2)
U-Bahn Herrengasse
☎ 513 82 94
Open Mon.-Fri. 10am-
6pm, Sat. 10am-5pm.**

This has become a cult shop where anyone who is anyone should buy his or her calfskin suitcase. The detail and finishing are impeccable, and the Tyrolean handbag made of

leather and *loden* converts into a tiny bag for just ATS4,000. The briefcases are lined in green silk, and the fine wallets (ATS1,500) are available in a range of five lovely colours - beige, yellow, red, dark green and ochre.

Hartmann

**Singerstrasse, 8 (C3)
U-Bahn Stephansplatz
☎ 512 14 89
Open Mon.-Fri. 10am-6pm,
Sat. 10am-5pm.**

Erich Hartmann is a craftsman who designs wonderful spectacle frames, made exclusively of buffalo and ox horn. He also makes combs, hair clips, bracelets, buttons and small brushes (ATS795). All his accessories are original and unique to this shop, and all fine examples of Austrian expertise and attention to detail. His shop is equally elegant with parquet flooring and white walls. Don't miss the lovely staircase resembling a church pulpit. Shopping here is a delight, and if you're looking for something really different to take home as a present, this is the place to come.

Michaela E. Lange

Piaristengasse, 5-7 (not on map)
U-Bahn Lerchenfelder Strasse
☎ 406 56 94
Open Mon.-Sat. 10am-6pm.

Having studied Applied Arts and been shortlisted in the Austrian Design Institute's national competition, this young fashion designer is passionate about women's hats. In summer she constructs her *Strohhüte*, straw hats in weird and wonderful shapes. In winter she moulds tall cylindrical felt hats for around ATS2,500, which she presents in the 'zen' section of her showroom.

THE KISS OF LIFE FOR HANDBAGS

If your suede bag is looking rather sad, hold it above a pan of boiling water and brush it with a special suede brush. If it's shiny, polish it with the cream at the top of fresh milk. If rain has stained the leather, give it a quick rub with a cloth dipped in 90% alcohol. If it's made of crocodile skin, protect it with a spray for reptile leather. If it was an expensive buy for a special occasion, it's better to take it to a leather expert to be revived, waterproofed or given new handles if so required.

Her bright, energetic window displays are a welcome change from the somewhat gloomy shops of the Josefstadt district. Hats off to her!

Schullin & Seitner

Kohlmarkt, 7 (B2)
U-Bahn Herrengasse
☎ 533 90 07
Open Mon.-Fri. 10am-6pm, Sat. 10am-5pm.

Even if you've no intention (or means) of buying anything in this wonderful emporium, you should treat yourself to a few moments of pleasure inside. The jewellery is contemporary in design and made with breathtaking precision, using metals and precious stones. Influenced by collaboration with the architect Hans Hollein in 1982, the designs have similarly pure, clean, and geometric lines. The platinum ring with sapphire

and aquamarine stones by Herbert Schullin is a fine example of this, as is his opal brooch in 16.09 carat gold (ATS44,000). Even if you don't purchase anything you can still dream.

Ernst A. Haban

Kärntnerstrasse, 16 (B3)
U-Bahn Stephansplatz
☎ 512 71 03
Open Mon.-Fri. 10am-6.30pm, Sat. 10am-5pm.

Ernst Haban's jewellery is classic in design, mostly Austrian and really superb. The prices are reasonable too, and you'll find really pretty, little delicate earrings and heart necklaces (ATS15,850).

Kecksilber

Bäckerstrasse, 10 (C2)
U-Bahn Stephansplatz
☎ 513 56 64
Open Mon.-Fri. 10am-6pm, Sat. 10am-5pm.

Walter Keck is a jeweller in a class all of his own. He's a magician with metal, and his creations are less expensive but just as inspirational as those of Schullin. His designs are very modern and extremely popular with the chic, young Viennese and the intelligentsia, especially his unique earrings (ATS350) and H-shaped necklaces (ATS1,560). If you treat yourself to a little accessory here you're sure to be noticed when you get home.

LINGERIE

If the number of lingerie shops in any given street is anything to go by, then it seems the Viennese are rather partial to their negligés, silk nightwear and other pretty *Unterwäsche* (underwear) with lace edges. Flimsy, frilly, flirty, flowery (or even flannelette) – whatever your heart's desire, Vienna will fill it.

Huber

Singerstrasse, 5 (C3)
U-Bahn Stephansplatz
☎ **512 97 62**
Open Mon.-Fri. 9.30am-7pm, Sat. 9.30am-5pm.

At Huber the emphasis is on sensible, comfortable and practical. They sell a huge selection of long johns, which are very necessary on cold nights in Vienna, when temperatures can take a dramatic tumble. They have attractive pyjamas with checks for women (ATS499) and stripes for men (ATS699). Children's pyjamas have little bears on them and are hypoallergenic. There's also a section of sporty 'bodywear', including the Skiny and Hanro labels, together with an interesting selection of elegant outfits for those dedicated to the art of serious aerobics.

Palmers

Kärntnerstrasse, 22 (B3)
U-Bahn Stephansplatz
☎ **512 24 95**
Open Mon.-Fri. 9.30am-7pm, Sat. 9.30am-5pm.

The styles are more exciting in this shop, but not 'over the top'. Palmers is a chain with shops throughout Austria and claims to be the 'guardian of classic femininity' in Vienna. There are three outlets in Kärntnerstrasse, selling attractive, glamorous and seductive lingerie. They have silk bustiers with pretty lace edges in ivory, beige and mother-of-pearl, which you can wear in the evenings under a low-cut jacket.

P2

Rotenturmstrasse, 23 (C2)
U-Bahn Stephansplatz
☎ **22 36 635 00 361**
Open Mon.-Fri. 10am-6.30pm, Sat. 10am-5pm.

This is a subsidiary of Palmers with three outlets in Vienna. It has recently launched a new lingerie line, called 'Lifestyle', which is aimed at young people interested in making a fashion statement. The prices are reasonable, and the designs a clever and contemporary mix of fitness and fun, with subtle but deliberate use of transparency. The see-through slips have been extremely popular, as have their stockings and tights at ATS59 and their pretty bras and tops at ATS169. The Viennese empty the shelves almost as quickly as they are filled in this shop. It's definitely worth a visit if you're looking for fun, practical lingerie at affordable places.

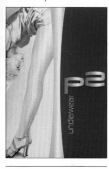

Galerie Macho

Bauermarkt, 2a (C2)
U-Bahn Stephansplatz
☎ 535 88 01
Open Mon.-Fri. 10am-6.30pm, Sat. 10am-5pm.

If you're looking for something pretty or cuddly to wear in the evening, you're in the right place. Everything in this shop is luxurious and voluptuous, with sophisticated dressing gowns and petticoats by designers such as

POLLSIRI

Kirchengasse, 25
(not on map)
U-Bahn Volkstheater
☎ 52 66 047
Open Mon.-Fri. 9am-1pm, 2-6pm, Sat. by appt.

This is the place to come if you know exactly what you want. Patrizia and Iris will make personalised boxer shorts (ATS340) and made-to-measure pyjamas (ATS2,100) in the fabric of your choice. You can even bring your own sample with you to have copied in their workshop. There's also a ready-to-wear collection, with prices ranging from ATS298-1,800.

Gianfranco Ferrè, Arturo Veneziani and Lucrezia Borgia. Fabrics used include silk, satin and brocade, and the lingerie is figure-hugging and even partially transparent, with lovely decorative touches. Their underwired bra in a pretty

leaf pattern (ATS1,180) would make a special souvenir to take home.

Adam underwear

Amerlingstrasse, 15
(not on map)
U-Bahn Neubaugasse
☎ 664 336 11 95
Open Mon.-Fri. 11am-7pm, Sat. 11am-5pm.

This shop was opened in 1996 and named Adam because of its rather masculine underwear, promoted with enthusiasm and commitment by Barbara, the owner. It's her mission to bring something new and unconventional to the world of underwear. You'll find the latest names in cheeky lingerie alongside the big boys, Calvin Klein, Nikos, Gigio Perla, Body Art and Olaf Benz. It's an interesting little shop to pop into, and you may emerge with something surprising.

Tiberius

Lindengasse, 2
(not on map)
U-Bahn Babenbergerstrasse
☎ 522 04 74
Open Mon.-Fri. 3-6pm, Sat. 11am-3pm.

If frilly lingerie is not your thing, head for Tiberius, which specialises in more serious materials, such as latex and leather. The items are made-to-measure and they'll kit you out from head to toe just as traditional tailors would do in days gone by. You may find there are rather too many laces to undo, but that's the price you have to pay for the latest look.

TRACHTENMODE: TRADITIONAL ALPINE COSTUME

Traditional Austrian dress is still popular in Austria. Rural in origin, and based on peasant and hunting costume, it's comfortable and practical, and you could happily buy and wear certain elements of it. Just be careful not to match the leather shorts with a Lacoste polo shirt, or you could provoke an embarrassing diplomatic incident.

girls with long hair wanting the 'Heidi' look. There are woollen capes, velvet boleros and men's jackets with embroidered collars (ATS1,600). It doesn't get much more bucolic than this – you'll feel you've just stepped into the country. Come here for 'The Sound of Music' look and your *Tracht* gifts to take home.

Loden Plankl

Michaelerplatz, 6 (B2)
U-Bahn Herrengasse
☎ 533 80 32
Open Mon.-Fri. 10am-6.30pm, Sat. 10am-5pm.

You simply can't miss this shop, situated just opposite the Hofburg. It has a huge selection of loden

coats (from ATS4,400), knitted socks with edelweisses embroidered on the side (from ATS370-460)

Tostmann

Schottengasse, 31 (A1)
U-Bahn Schottentor
☎ 533 53 31
Open Mon.-Fri., 10am-6.30pm, Sat. 10am-5pm.

You'll discover authentic and rather touching *Trachten* in this shop, with its pale parquet flooring and painted furniture. Entire families are dressed in traditional costume from head to toe here, and there are armfuls of pretty dresses (ATS4,300), aprons and floral shirt fronts for young

depending on length and design) and shirts that are still worn in the Alps to this day, with a little charm, such as a boar's snout or a squirrel's foot, on a chain. If you've been longing for a loden coat, you're in the right shop.

LODEN

Even though lodens are made of merino wool nowadays, the ample coats that allowed the Tyrolean shepherds to stride out on the mountains still retain their wonderful insulating properties. Protective in all weathers, they're highly practical and stylish. The manufacturers have given names to the four types of loden, depending on the strength and roughness of the fabric – *Tuch-*, *Sämisch-*, *Doubleface-* and *Strichloden.*

Resi Hammerer

Kärntnerstrasse, 29-31 (B3)
U-Bahn Stephansplatz
☎ 512 69 52
Open Mon.-Fri. 10am-6.30pm, Sat. 10am-5pm.

Two floors of *Trachtenmode* and haute couture are here, with the creations Austrian designers, including Admont, Gaisberger and Lodenfrey hanging side by side with those of international fashion houses and Resi's own collection. An ex-skier on the national team, Resi is an expert in loden design and in the juxtaposition of colour and fabric There are some lovely chine jumpers by Maria di Ripabianca, pretty cashmere shawls, woollen jackets with suede collars and quilted velvet jackets. This is a great shop to browse in if you're not in the mood for serious buying.

Eduard Kettner

Seilergasse, 12 (B2)
☎ 513 22 39
Open Mon.-Fri. 10am-6.30pm, Sat. 10am-5pm.

The clothes here have the 'hunting and walking' look, with suede jackets in autumnal shades. The lapels have an oak-leaf emblem on them, and the overall look is very smart.

Habsburg

Kärntnerstrasse, 19 (B3)
U-Bahn Stephansplatz
☎ 513 06 80
Open Mon.-Fri. 9.30am-7pm, Sat. 9.30am-5pm.

If you're hankering after imperial days, head for the fourth floor of the Steffl department store, where the original aristocratic and neo-Romantic *Trachtenmode* is on sale in the 'Casual & Country' section. The Schneiders from Salzburg launched the collection in 1992, with the support of Francesca von Habsburg, and it has been a commercial success due to the quality and cut of the fabrics. Each model carries the name of a member of the imperial family: Maria Leopoldine, Hildegard, Balthasar, etc. A tundra waistcoat will cost ATS3,390 and a jacket with buttons made from antlers will set you back ATS9,990.

Lanz

Kärntnerstrasse, 10 (B3)
U-Bahn Stephansplatz
☎ 512 24 56
Open Mon.-Fri. 9.30am-6pm, Sat. 9.30am-5pm.

Since 1922, Lanz has been creating clothes that are more

'Habsburg' in style than high fashion, but that still respect traditional methods and design. Available in hunting green, brown and charcoal grey, the clothes retain their rustic look, but with a softer line. You'll find the key components of a *Tracht* wardrobe here – *Dirndl, Lederhosen* and *Walkjanker.*

Sportalm

Haas-Haus
Stephansplatz, 12 (C2)
U-Bahn Stephansplatz
☎ 535 52 89
Open Mon.-Fri. 10am-6.30pm, Sat. 10am-5pm.

This fashion designer from Kitzbühel is in a class of his own with his version of *Trachtenmode.* He has adapted the traditional clothes to suit modern-day city living, using new fabrics for designs inspired by the original *Joppe* (jacket) and *Walkjanker* (coat) worn by the Tyrolean shepherds. The result is an attractive, slightly yuppy or preppy range in grey, cream and natural colours that's perfect for formal evenings.

FROM HEAD TO TOE

You'd be very much mistaken if you thought that Viennese shoemakers were only experts in snow shoes and walking boots. They also make lovely court shoes, Oxford shoes in Russian leather and kid boots, paying great attention to comfort and detail. With our help, you should be able to find the perfect pair to go to the ball, the beach or the latest trendy café.

Kurt Denkstein
Bauernmarkt, 8 (C2)
U-Bahn Stephansplatz
☎ 533 04 60
Open Mon.-Fri. 10am-6.30pm, Sat. 10am-5pm.

Kurt Denkstein is a friendly shop where you can try on shoes to your heart's content in a relaxing atmosphere with music playing in the background. The selection of shoes is really impressive, and you should emerge with a spring in your step in a new pair. Try the 'Sunday in Venice' style (ATS1,990) or a pair of 'miumiu' in black (ATS2,700). All the major labels are here too - Sonia Rykiel, Robert Clergerie, Pitti and Gerardo Fossati. You'll enjoy looking very well-heeled.

Dominici
Singerstrasse, 2 (C3)
U-Bahn Stephansplatz
☎ 513 45 41
Open Mon.-Fri. 9.30am-7pm, Sat. 9.30am-5pm.

Dominici has its own mission statement for your feet – to supply the best, most practical and elegant footwear possible. The shoes are both sophisticated and comfortable, so you can happily wear them for cocktails at the Opera or for braving the elements on the pavements of the Ringstrasse. A pair of shoes by Mario Rapagnani or Dominici uomo will set you back ATS1,950.

Ludwig Reiter
Wiedner Haupstrasse, 41 (not on map)
U-Bahn Taubstummengasse
☎ 505 82 58
Open Mon.-Fri. 10am-6pm, Sat. 10am-5pm.

This is one of Vienna's top shoe shops. It has been famous since 1885 for its sophisticated designs, double stitching, the superb quality of its leather and the effectiveness of its own wax products. Reiter lovingly puts the finishing touches to his traditional designs, known as the 'Wiener' and 'Theresianer' and is renowned for his sturdy winter footwear. His comfortable but strong *Maronibrater* are ideal for walks in the Alps, and smart enough, in cognac or moccha fur-lined leather, for an opening night at the Burgtheater. A pair of 'Gustav Mahler' or 'Pater Brown' shoes will last you more than ten years, so it's worth investing in a pair at this shop or at the other outlet at Moelkersteig, 1, U-Bahn Schottentor, ☎ 533 42 04.

Zak
Kärntnerstrasse, 36 (B3)
U-Bahn Stephansplatz
☎ 512 72 57
Open Mon.-Fri. 10am-6pm, Sat. 10am-5pm.

Since 1912, four generations of the Zak family have contributed to the company's expertise in the choice of leather and perfect finishes. The elegant women's shoes from the workshops of Casadei, Sergio Rossi, Pollini and other Italians, and men's classic

designs made by Zak itself are displayed in an elegant neo-Jugendstil showroom. Hand-sewn evening shoes in black patent leather are available for ATS3,400, with the timeless *'Norweger'* design costing ATS4,900, and the *'Budapester'* shoe still going strong.

Humanic

**Mariahilferstrasse, 1b
(not on map)
U-Bahn Rabenberger Strasse
☎ 587 41 58
Open Mon.-Fri. 10am-6.30pm, Sat. 10am-5pm.**

You couldn't fail to find the perfect fit at this store, designed by Boris Pedrecca. The range includes moccasins, 'ankle boots', cowboy boots, sports shoes and all the top label fashion boots, aimed at a young and sporty clientèle. The prices are reasonable, and the fashions are the latest to be seen walking the catwalk and the pavements of Mariahilferstrasse. Humanic is well known within Austria for its surreal advertisements on TV.

Gerald Fischer

**Liechtensteinstrasse, 29
(not on map)
U-Bahn Schottentor
☎ 317 91 28
Open Mon.-Fri. 10am-6pm, Sat. 10am-1pm.**

Another district, another shoemaker, but this time you've entered the premises of a made-to-measure craftsman. Fischer can give the kiss of life to your favourite but tired-looking shoes or make you another pair, even from a photo. Prices start around ATS4,000, and you choose the type of leather and style.

R. Scheer and Söhne

**Bräunerstrasse 4 (B2)
U-Bahn Stephansplatz
☎ 533 80 84
Open Mon.-Fri. 10am-6.30pm, Sat. 10am-5pm.**

Former court shoemaker and medal winner in the 1873 Universal Exhibition, this company cuts and sews each boot by hand, in accordance with traditional royal and imperial methods. The boots fit as smoothly as a pair of gloves, and they'll last you a long time.

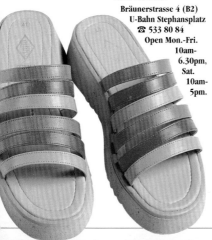

KIDS' CORNER

Children's fashions in Vienna tend to be sensible rather than terribly exciting. Your tiny treasures may not find their favourite labels in the shops, but they may fall for a little shirt or parka that will be the envy of their friends when they get home. Solve that early morning 'nothing to wear today' crisis once and for all. You'll also find some lovely toys.

Mimi

Krugerstrasse, 10 (B3)
U-Bahn Stephansplatz
☎ 512 43 18
Open Mon.-Fri. 10am-6pm,
Sat. 10am-5pm.

You'll find a range of cleverly designed clothes for babies and toddlers here. The collection by a Milanese designer is an attractive mix of imagination, practicality

and comfort in rather classic styles. There are pretty green polo tops for 2-year-olds (ATS495), fleece-lined Valtherm jackets for cold winter days (ATS2,395) and sweet little Irlandia dresses (ATS1,395). This is a lovely shop to browse in, even if you're not in the mood for buying something for the little treasures.

Albicocco

Strozzigasse, 32
(not on map)
U-Bahn Lerchenfelder
Strasse
☎ 408 99 20
Open Mon.-Fri. 10am-
6pm, Sat. 10am-1pm.

This shop is a little out of the way but it's worth the journey, as the prices are excellent and the clothes practical and hard-wearing. They're mainly imported from Italy and Holland and hang from the branches of an apricot tree. You'll find colourful sweatshirts for ATS350 and little Catimini hats in natural colours. The clothes range is for newborns to 14-year-olds and makes a welcome change from the predictable pink and blue designs found elsewhere.

Taki-To

Petersplatz, 8 (B2)
U-Bahn
Stephansplatz
☎ 535 18 23
Open Mon.-Fri. 10am-
6pm, Sat. 10.30am-
4.30pm.

The Viennese designer behind the Taki-To name came up with the

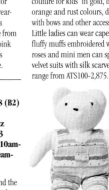

idea of an entire range of imaginative jackets and dresses for holidays and special occasions. His concept was 'haute couture for kids' in gold, brown, orange and rust colours, decorated with bows and other accessories. Little ladies can wear capes with fluffy muffs embroidered with tiny roses and mini men can sport velvet suits with silk scarves. Prices range from ATS100-2,875.

BABY SITTING AND KIDS' CLUB

If you're looking for someone to look after your children for a few hours you can call **Bambina** on 0664 301 39 33, but make sure you book a couple of days in advance. There are also the **Viennese Babysitters**, whom you can contact on ☎ 587 35 25 and 408 70 46. For children aged 4 to 12 call **Zoom** on ☎ 522 67 48. They're based in the Museum district (U-Bahn Babenbergerstrasse), and they have an interesting programme of activities, including exhibitions and workshops. They charge ATS50 per child.

Spielzeugschachtel

Rauhensteingasse, 5 (C3)
U-Bahn Stephansplatz
☎ 512 44 94
Open Mon.-Fri. 10am-
6.30pm, Sat. 10am-5pm.

The 'Toy Box' is a children's paradise, but plenty of adults seem to enjoy the magnificent toys just as much. The shop has banned plastic toys, guns, monsters and violent games and stocks only beautiful wooden objects, aimed at improving children's skills in reasoning, observation and understanding. A good example is the delightful mosaic of coloured cubes invented by Kathrin Kiener (ATS1,280). You'll find jigsaws, children's books, fluffy toys, dolls, the complete collection of Ravensburger puzzles, a giant giraffe construction kit and the famous Pampolina dolls by Gotz.

Kober

Graben, 14-15 (B2)
U-Bahn Stephansplatz
☎ 533 60 18
Open Mon.-Fri. 10am-
6.30pm.

Wandering round Kober will feel like stepping back into your childhood. This narrow shop founded in 1868 is brimming with lead soldiers, models, games and Steiff teddy bears. The special guest star is the little green dragon, Tabaluga, who is the hero of a German television series. There are electric trains made by the Austrian company Fleischmann, together with their many accessories. You can spend many a happy hour here.

Das Kinderhaus

Mariahilfer Strasse, 1c
(not on map)
U-Bahn Babenbergerstrasse
☎ 587 61 54
Open Mon.-Fri. 10am-
6pm, Sat. 10am-1pm.

If you're decorating your children's rooms, this is the place to come. Even if there's no room left in your suitcase, you'll find plenty of inspiration in the form of space-saving, educational or fun furniture. Everything is well made and highly practical, including C-shaped tables with holes,

slots and grooves, chairs that look like trees, and wardrobes disguised as houses, all in vibrant colours, which include canary yellow, fire engine red, Kermit green and kingfisher blue.

Schuhhaus zur Oper

Tegetthoffstrasse, 5 (B3)
U-Bahn Stephansplatz
☎ 512 47 79
Open Mon.-Fri. 10am-6pm,
Sat. 10am-1pm.

Just a stone's throw from the Opera there's a shop with a huge selection of shoes for little feet, designed by Elefanten, Naturino and Giesswein. There are practical, fun, hard-wearing, very light and very flexible models, with prices ranging from ATS799 to ATS1,099 according to size. There are more classic designs in wool for very small feet.

INTERIOR DESIGN AND TABLEWARE

Whether you're looking for antiques (a Jugendstil bowl, some '*Maria-Theresia*' porcelain or a Biedermeier console table) or hi-tech gadgets for the home, Vienna won't disappoint you. Go along to one of the places below to find that special item belonging to the last century or the next. You'll learn more about what it's really like to live in Vienna.

LAMPS

Woka

Singerstrasse, 16 (C3)
U-Bahn Stephansplatz
☎ 513 29 12
Open Mon.-Fri. 11am-6pm, Sat. 10am-5pm.

Wolfgang Karolinsky, alias 'Woka', came up with the clever idea of buying back from the suppliers to the Austrian monarchy all the machinery used until 1932 to make the wonderful lamps by Josef Hoffman and Otto Wagner. He now makes faithful reproductions in a choice of solid, nickel-plated or lacquered brass. Next to these lovely models you'll find seductive works by contemporary designers, including Matteo Thun and Harry Gluck. Prices start at AS13,000.

Nanu

Josefstädter Strasse, 44
(not on map)

U-Bahn Rathaus
☎ 406 25 28
Open Mon.-Fri. 10am-6pm, Sat. 10am-3pm.

Gernot Manske and Walter Pangerl have shed light on the subject by creating a minimalist system, called the 'Cubic,' with lampshades in a variety of materials, including silk, paper, glass, aluminium and brass and in a choice of colours. Futuristic and industrial in design, they're perfect for that loft you're thinking of moving into. Prices range from ATS1,686 to ATS2,490.

DESIGN

Henn

Naglergasse, 29 (B2)
U-Bahn Herrengasse
☎ 533 83 82
Open Mon.-Fri. 9am-6.30-pm, Sat. 9am-5pm.

Be warned – you're very unlikely to emerge empty-handed from this shop. Hartmann Henn has wonderful furniture and accessories for the home, all of them simply irresistible. He sells stoneware salad bowls patterned with white flowers (ATS195), espresso machines (ATS5,990) and a huge variety of modern gadgets for trendy folk who don't take themselves too seriously.

Der graue Rabe fliegt

**Piaristengasse, 1
(not on map)
U-Bahn Lerchenfelder
Strasse
☎ 406 94 89
Open Mon.-Fri. 10am-6pm,
Sat. 10am-1pm.**

'The Flying Grey Raven' is a showroom full of surprises that you shouldn't miss. Erwin Ebenberger displays his own designs, as well as those of Peter Rohde, including revolving cupboards and other interesting storage ideas. The furniture is made of eco-friendly and recyclable materials, and pieces can be juxtaposed or placed at a variety of angles, depending on their function. There are smaller items that you'll be able to fit more easily into your suitcase, such as plates (ATS990) and bowls fired at very high temperatures by Martin Zwölfer, an Austrian ceramic artist who trained in Japan.

Quas

**Gumpendorferstrasse 16
U-Bahn Babenbergerstrasse
☎ 586 23 56
Open Mon.-Fri. 10am-6pm,
Sat. 10am-4pm.**

The Quas team's mission is to create and conquer space while retaining harmony and style. Their showroom is filled with chamber music, furnishing fabric designed by Sahco and Zimmer & Rhode, beautiful, simple chests and stunning wardrobes by Dell'Orto & Cattaneo. The collection seems to launch your home into the third millenium – at a price. A maple chair costs ATS5,427 and a display cabinet will set you back ATS41,242.

GLASS AND PORCELAIN

Lobmeyr

**Kärntnerstrasse, 26 (B3)
U-Bahn Stephansplatz
☎ 512 05 08
Open Mon.-Fri. 9am-
6.30pm, Sat. 9am-5pm.**

This famous glass manufacturer was founded in 1823, and the glassware is still made to the neo-Baroque and neo-Renaissance designs of the 19th century. On the glass shelves of this lovely shop you'll find the most beautiful crystal in Vienna, together with delicate hand-painted Herend porcelain (ATS700-3,000). There are also pieces based on original designs by Adolf Loos, such as his 1929 decanter (ATS12,682), and by Josef Hoffmann. The best-selling designs include the *'Musselinglas'* (1856), Paul Wieser's 'Ballerina' (1992) and Jeronim Tisljar's 'Floppy Disc' glasses (ATS618). The museum on the top floor has a small exhibition of Lobmeyr's early work.

Augarten

**Stock im Eisen-Platz, 3 (B2)
U-Bahn Stephansplatz
☎ 512 14 94
Open Mon.-Fri. 9.30am-
6pm, Sat. 9.30am-5pm.**

Augarten is the Rolls Royce of Austrian porcelain manufacturers. The *'Maria-Theresia'* design, with

its pretty green patterns, was a great success (each plate cost ATS1700), which was then matched by that of the *'Wiener Rose'* (Viennese Rose), with its green border. The company has now launched two neo-Classical services with 33 pieces each that are perfect for an important dinner. The 'Elisabeth' service is based on the one used by Emperor Ferdinand, and the 'Courage' service has a black background with red patterns. These must be washed with care as the gold is very fragile. You can also buy direct from the factory (see p. 66).

Interio

**Mariahilferstrasse, 19-21
(not on map)
U-Bahn Babenbergerstrasse
☎ 585 17 31
Open Mon.-Fri. 10am-7pm,
Sat. 9am-5pm.**

Try to imagine a furniture shop
somewhere between Habitat,
Conran and Ikea. That's Interio,
which has simple, practical,
flexible and modern designs at
reasonable prices. You'll find
sisal rugs, curtains and an
attractive range of cushions by
Carasso in 13 different colours
(ATS179). Interio offers terrific
choice at good prices – an
excellent combination.

Karner & Karner

**Siebensterngasse, 4 (not
on map)
U-Bahn Volkstheater
☎ 524 40 28
Open Mon.-Fri.
10am-6pm, Sat.
10am-3pm.**

This shop with its
white textured walls
and pale wooden
floors is in the
Spittelberg district. It
has an interesting
and eclectic range of
items for the table and
home, including throws,
tables and vases from places
as far apart as New York and
Java. It's a great place for
inspiration.

Thonet

**Kohlmarkt, 6 (B2)
U-Bahn Herrengasse
☎ 533 77 88
Open Mon.-Fri.
10am-6.30pm, Sat.
10am-5pm.**

Thonet were originally
manufacturers of very
competitively-priced furniture
that was sold throughout the
Austro-Hungarian Empire.
People queued to buy their
rocking-chair or chaise-longue
made with a revolutionary
bentwood technique. The
famous 'No 14 Chair' was
amazingly successful, with
45 million sold between 1859
and 1900. It's still there
alongside other 'sitting
machines' (ATS2,500), tables
and display cabinets in
myrtle wood (ATS84,360).
Thonet's products are now
collector's items, and they
make furniture to order.
You might like to
commission something,
or buy one of their hat
stands and have it
delivered home to avoid
sharing a seat with it on
the plane!

TABLEWARE

Haardt & Krüger

**Schottengasse, 3a (A1)
U-Bahn Schottentor
☎ 533 73 29
Open Mon.-Fri., 9am-6pm,
Sat. 9am-5pm.**

The doors of Haardt & Krüger
first opened in 1875, and
today the shop is still one of
the first choices for wedding
lists. There are some very
typically Austrian items for
sale, such as bread boxes and
chopping boards with inlaid
wood by Mitheis (ATS368), as
well as international products –
cutlery by Alessi, candlesticks by the
Swedish designer Bengt Lindberg
(ATS231), Emilio Bergamin's
rather comical plates and a new

array of casserole dishes and pans, humorous Bohemian crystal vases (ATS159-209), beer glasses by Ritzenhoff and a whole range of tableware, including some particularly pretty plates by the German designer Hutschenreuther, with a green leaf and yellow flower pattern. Equally attractive are the coffee cups by Countess Lene von Thun, decorated with moon and cloud motifs. Prices for these gifts start at ATS290.

Kunst & Kram
Bauernmarkt, 11-13 (C2)
U-Bahn Stephansplatz
☎ 535 96 52
Open Mon.-Fri. 10am-6.30pm, Sat. 10am-6pm.

Karin Kecht is full of imagination the result is a display of some wonderfully creative tableware. There's a lovely assortment of silver cutlery, guaranteed until 2021, pretty green glasses with

generation of stylish and very practical spoons called 'Rösle' which have a ring at the end.

Thun-Hohenstein
Wollzeile, 26 (C2)
U-Bahn Stephansplatz
☎ 512 54 61
Open Mon.-Fri. 10am-6.30pm, Sat. 10am-5pm.

On the four floors of this family-run shop you'll come across an

HUNGARIAN PORCELAIN

Much of the porcelain in Vienna comes from Hungarian manufacturers, principally Herend and Zsolnay. Herend was founded in 1813 and still produces porcelain of the utmost delicacy with a rose motif inspired by Meissen and Sèvres. Zsolnay has been making ivory-coloured porcelain since 1851, but it's lost some of the style it had in the Art Nouveau period. Pieces from this era are beautiful but hard to find. You can recognise Hollóháza porcelain by the little green flowers on a white background.

gold polka dots from Orrefors in Sweden (ATS3,198 each) and small Castanetti candles made in Vienna. If you're looking for decorative ideas you need go no further. Karin's collection is a subtle mixture of original local products and some stunning international designs.

ANTIQUES AND COLLECTIBLES

There's no point scouring the whole of Vienna in the hope of finding an Ottoman shield or an Art Deco decanter. The antique shops are concentrated in just two or three streets around the Dorotheum, between Spiegelgasse and Bräunerstrasse. This is the area to wander round and we've selected a few places for you to visit. If, however, you find the prices a little off-putting, head for the Wollzeile or Fleischmarkt area, where they are more reasonable.

E. M. Mautner

Herrengasse, 2 (A/B2)
U-Bahn Herrengasse
☎ 533 12 24
Open Mon.-Fri. 10am-6pm, Sat. 10am-1pm.

For a long time Vienna was the veritable hub of the art world in Central Europe and the former Soviet Union. Many works passed through the Austrian capital, including some whose authenticity has been put in doubt. There's no need to worry in this shop, though – all the charming little pictures decorating the walls of Melch Mautner are authentic icons from 19th-century Russia, with prices starting at ATS4,000.

Bauernfeind

Dorotheergasse, 9 (B3)
U-Bahn Stephansplatz
☎ 513 10 20
Open Mon.-Fri. 10am-6pm, Sat. 10am-1pm.

Bauernfeind isn't one of those antique shops that simply arranges rows of Voltaire chairs or Biedermeier chests of drawers in

Alfred Kolhammer

Dorotheergasse, 15 (B3)
U-Bahn Stephansplatz
☎ 513 20 63
Open Mon.-Fri. 10am-6pm, Sat. 10am-1pm.

This antique dealer, renowned for his professionalism, has some rather large and expensive pieces in his shop. His early 18th-century Madonna statues from Salzburg are as cumbersome as they're priceless. However, if you have a smaller home (and wallet), there are some lovely naïve paintings and pretty rustic furniture in painted wood to tempt you. Have a good browse.

chic surroundings. Every item is selected with great taste and beautifully displayed. A late 16th-century majolica dish from Urbino will set you back ATS52,000.

Galerie am Lobkowitz-Platz

Lobkowitz-Platz (B3)
U-Bahn Stephansplatz
☎ 512 13 38
Open Mon.-Fri. 10am-1pm, 3-6pm.

At Ursula Farda's shop you'll find 18th-century paintings alongside golden angel wings and works by Viennese landscape artists, such as Leopold Vöscher (1830-1877), whose art has become very popular recently. Ursula Farda's collection is one of the most impressive in the field and a delight for all lovers of antiques.

TIPS ON HOW TO TAKE CARE OF YOUR SILVERWARE

If the silver cutlery you buy is looking a little tired and rather dowdy, it's time to get to work with the silver polish. If there are stubborn rust stains, rub the silver with a piece of cotton wool dipped in water and bicarbonate of soda or with a toothbrush dipped in caustic soda. Finally, polish with whitening. Your silverware should be bright and gleaming once more.

Wissenschaftliches Kabinett

Spiegelgasse 23 (B3)
U-Bahn Stephansplatz
☎ 512 41 26
Open Mon.-Fri. 4-6pm
Saturday by appointment.

This is the only antique shop in Vienna specialising in astronomical and surgical instruments. Instead of the usual antique items, you'll find sextants, telescopes, apothecary's phials and old scalpels. It's well worth a look round if you're at all scientifically inclined.

Bric à Brac

Habsburggasse, 9 (B2)
U-Bahn Stephansplatz
☎ 533 60 26
Open Mon.-Fri. 10am-1pm, 2-6pm, Sat. 10am-noon.

Bric à Brac will transport you to another era, with a collection of streamlined chrome, tapered shapes and smooth surfaces. Lovers of Bakelite will head straight for the lamps and then find all sorts of household items from 1935 to 1965. There are toasters, juicers, mixers and shakers, and all you need is a Cadillac to take them home in.

Chronothek Gunczy

Braunerstrasse, 8 (B2)
U-Bahn Stephansplatz
☎ 532 05 49
Open Mon.-Fri. 11am-6pm, Sat. 10am-4pm.

This is the place to come if you're planning to spend every schilling you possess on an almost antique watch. Gunczy has a huge selection of wonderful time-pieces, such as the IWC Porsche Design Sportivo (ATS18,650) and the Ulysse Nardin from the 1940s (ATS35,000). You'll be the envy of all watch collectors with either of these superb items, so pop in if you're in the market for a pocket-sized work of art.

Uhren-, Schmuck- und Antiquitätenbörse

Operngasse, 10
(not on map)
U-Bahn Karlsplatz
☎ 587 83 33
Open Mon.-Fri. 10am-7pm, Sat. 9am-3pm.

Kurt Nachtmann is in charge of this small antique shop, and has watches, clocks and jewellery for sale, among other items. Kurt is passionate about watches, and in the window you're likely to find anything from 1910 models or a 1945 Omega watch for ATS5,000 to a rare Breitling 'Navitiner Cosmonaut' from 1961 that will set you back ATS21,900. If you have time (and money) on your hands, this is the place to spend it. You'll find some really impressive time-pieces in the cabinets.

FURNITURE AND OBJECTS FROM DISTANT LANDS

It was once said that Vienna was the gateway to the Orient, and as you wander round the shops, you'll be tempted to agree it still is. The range of exotic items on offer is fascinating, from saris, batik fabric, Anatolian kilims, and necklaces from the Atlas mountains to lacquered furniture from China. We've selected some of the most interesting shops for you to visit on your trip to the East.

Die Karawane

Sonnenfelsgasse, 1 (C2)
U-Bahn Stephansplatz
☎ **513 19 66**
Open Tue.-Fri. 11.30am-7.30pm, Sat. 10am-5pm.

This tiny shop looks like a mixture of a Moorish interior and a Moroccan souk. In it are beautiful ceramics from Safi, Berber rugs (from ATS1,500), Turkish slippers and leather lampshades painted with henna (ATS700).

India

Strobelgsse, 2 (C2)
U-Bahn Stephansplatz
☎ **512 51 96**
Open Tue.-Fri., 10am-6pm, Sat. 10am-5pm.

Come here and you'll think you've been transported to an exotic,

Adil Besim

Graben, 30 (B2)
U-Bahn Stephansplatz
tel 533 09 10
Open Mon.-Fri. 9.30am-6pm,
Sat. 9.30am-5pm.

After a short journey in the lift you'll find yourself in the den of the best carpet dealer in Austria. Ferdi Besim has more than 10,000 stunning rugs and carpets and will spend as much time as you need explaining the origins of each, the technique used in its manufacture and the various colour combinations possible. The most sought-after models start at around ATS475,000, but don't be put off by this price tag. A lovely 'Heriz Bachschayesch' rug in green or gold costs only ATS8,000, and if you're only interested in modern carpets, there are some lovely contemporary designs in Tibetan wool by Stephanie Odegard.

distant land. You'll need much more than just a morning in order to explore all Pravin K Cherkoori's metal containers which are literally overflowing with beautiful organza, brocade and cashmere from India. Inside the shop, you'll find pretty embroidered caftans (ATS1,895) and short taffeta jackets in a rich red colour (ATS6,597). In 'India' you'll find all the fabrics, accessories and inspiration you will need if you dream of transforming your bedroom at home into an exotic boudoir or yourself into an alluring Maharajah.

Rieger Gallery
Morzimplatz, 4 (C1)
☎ 533 89 82
U-Bahn Schwedenplatz
Open Mon.-Sat. 10am-6pm.

The Rieger Gallery has the most African window display in Vienna. It has traditional crafts from across the length and breadth of the savanna that have now become decorative items. You'll find furniture painted with big cats and a treasure trove of gifts at reasonable prices, such as wooden mirrors in the shape of the sun (ATS299) or boxes covered in banana skins (ATS100). This is a great shop for unusual gifts.

Himalayan Arts
Kirchberggasse, 16
(not on map)
U-Bahn Volkstheater
☎ 523 29 67
Open Mon.-Sat. 2-7pm.

Himalyan Arts will tempt you away from the Spittelberg district with its selection of Nepalese and Tibetan pieces and contemplative music. There are silk paintings, local craft items and lots of sandalwood objects. The prices are reasonable, and you'll enjoy browsing in the relaxing, incense-filled atmosphere.

Studio Haas & Haas
Ertlgasse, 4 (C2)
U-Bahn Stephansplatz
☎ 533 35 34
Open Mon.-Sat. 10am-7pm.

If Frau Haas isn't to be found in her shop in Vienna, it's more than likely that she's scouring China for authentic furniture. When she returns to the Austrian capital, she displays her treasures with exquisite taste among the low tables and wall coverings of her studio.

Lotos
Schottnefeldgasse, 65
(not on map)
U-Bahn Burggasse
☎ 524 08 39
Open Mon.-Fri. 10am-7pm,
Sat. 10am-5pm.

This large depot tucked away in a courtyard in Neubau has an

> ### TWO WOODS –
> ### SANDAL AND BALSA
>
> Sandalwood comes from the Malabar Coast, Java and Indonesia, and, due to its smoothness and strength was used in the past in marquetry. It's a perfumed wood and today is used to make delicate honey-coloured or red boxes. Balsa wood comes from Central America and is the lightest wood in the world, the choice of makers of model of airplanes and 'DIY' enthusiasts. However, it is important to note that it's also relatively porous.

interesting assortment of objects, including sofas, fabric, place mats and wrought-iron accessories. It's an eclectic but tasteful collection from India with prices ranging from ATS3,000 for a small chest of drawers to ATS18,000 for a folding screen with Buddhist motifs. It's a wonderful place to browse.

BOOKS, CDS AND VIDEOS

Vienna has a huge number of bookshops but only a few selling English-language books. Our selection includes those that do, so you won't go home empty-handed. There are also many music shops to browse in, and those of you wanting to complete your collection of Mozart's music or the Viennese New Year concerts will be spoiled for choice. Music is still very much the passion of the Austrian capital and a vital part of the city's culture.

Emi Austria

Karntnerstrasse, 30 (B3)
U-Bahn Stephansplatz
☎ **512 36 75**
Open Mon.-Fri. 9.30am-6.30pm, Sat. 9.30am-5pm.

EMI is less exclusive than Gramola, and you'll find an eclectic selection of rock, jazz, world music and classical recordings. The top floor is dedicated to the latter, whereas the first two floors have traditional Austrian music and contemporary composers. Everything is impeccably ordered and clearly labelled, so you won't have any difficulty finding the lastest CD or Austro-Slovenian musical offering.

Prachner

Kärntnerstrasse, 30 (B3)
U-Bahn Stephansplatz
☎ **512 85 49**
Open Mon.-Fri. 9.30am-6.30pm, Sat. 9.30am-5pm.

The architect Gernot Mittersteiner

Gramola

Kohlmarkt, 5 (B2)
U-Bahn Herrengasse
☎ **533 50 47**
Open Mon.-Fri. 10am-6pm, Sat. 10am-5pm.

Gramola is a tiny temple to classical music and the favourite haunt of opera fans. If you're looking for a present for a music lover who has everything, this is the place to come. You'll find recordings produced by Naxos and the Russian label, Melodiya, together with live recordings from the National Opera in Vienna. The staff are experts on their stock and can give excellent advice on even the most obscure pieces. You can ask them anything – they'll be happy to help.

has given the windows of Prachner a whole new look. This is definitely the place to shop in Vienna, both for its excellent and extensive collection of books and its trendy decor. The sections on design, architecture and town planning are the best in Vienna, and there's an English section with guides to the city, together with travel books and novels. You'll find mountains of exhibition catalogues, a feast of books on Viennese monuments, and a collection of wonderful monographs on Austrian architects, such as Adolf Krischanitz.

Morawa

Wollzeile, 11 (C2)
U-Bahn Stephansplatz
☎ 515 62 450
Open Mon.-Fri. 9am-6pm,
Sat. 9am-5pm.

Morawa is a good general bookshop full of nooks and crannies. At the back of the store there's a huge selection of English and other foreign-language magazines and newspapers, together with a few guides to Vienna, while the English-language book section is on the first floor. You'll find novels and

guidebooks as well as books on architecture and photography, including the latest portfolio by the Viennese photographer, Andreas Bitesnich. This is a great place to come and browse.

Gilhofer

Bognergasse, 2 (B2)
U-Bahn Herrengasse
☎ 533 42 85

Open Mon.-Fri. 10am-1pm,
2-6pm,
Sat. 10am-1pm.

This highly respected bookshop is dedicated to antique books and prints. You'll have the opportunity to see views of 19th-century Vienna (ATS2,000), fashion plates and antique maps of the Austro-Hungarian empire (ATS4,500).

MUSIC SCORES

Gifted pianists and violinists wanting to spend some of their weekend in search of a Mozart minuet or rare opera libretto should come to Doblinger at Dorotheergasse, 10, (B3). The nearest station is U-Bahn Stephansplatz, and the shop is open Mon.- Fri. 9am-6pm, Sat. 9am-noon. Call them on ☎ 515 03 0 or fax your order through to them on 515 03 51, and they'll be happy to send out scores to you, both locally and internationally.

Satyr-Filmwelt

Marc-Aurel-Strasse, 5 (C1/2)
(entrance in Vorlaufstrasse)
U-Bahn Schwedenplatz
☎ 535 53 27
Open Mon.-Fri. 10am-
7.30pm, Sat. 9am-5pm.

Film buffs love this place, with its substantial collection of scripts, biographies, posters (ATS200), CD soundtracks and art-house videos in the original language. The shop is on two floors and should have just what you want if you're a dedicated cinemagoer. Some of the books are in English, French and German. It's paradise for screenlovers.

Black Market

1, Gonzagagasse, 9 (C1)
U-Bahn
Schottenring/Schwedenplatz
☎ 533 76 17
Open Mon.-Fri. 10am-
7.30pm, Sat. 10am-5pm.

This is the Viennese headquarters of dance music. If you're familiar with house, techno tribal, hip hop, funk, groove and soul music, you should get to know Black Market too. You never know, you may find that elusive CD you've been looking for. The adjoining café is the place to be seen, and streetwear and its accessories are de rigueur. Enjoy a browse in the shop followed by a coffee in one of Vienna's coolest spots.

SOUVENIRS AND SMALL GIFTS

If you enjoy buying presents to take home for friends and family, or if you want to buy yourself a few souvenirs to remind you of your wonderful weekend, there's plenty of scope in Vienna. Venture away from the major department stores into the 1st district and the Spittelberg quarter, where you'll come across some unique gifts. They may be funny, kitsch, even rather strange, but they are bound to be original.

Die vermischte Warenhandlung
Weihburggasse, 16 (C3)
U-Bahn Stephansplatz
☎ **512 88 53 15**
Open Mon.-Fri. 10am-6pm, Sat. 10am-5pm.

Don't wait until Christmas to have a good old rummage round Aichinger, Bernhard & Co. Their shop, with its interesting assortment of merchandise, is tucked away in a courtyard close to Franziskanerplatz. They have everything you could think of to decorate your home as well as your gifts, including ribbons and stunning wrapping paper. In addition, you'll find soft toys, cups, soaps, all sorts of boxes and phials, perfumed candles and silk flowers. The choice is so vast it will make you wonder where it comes from.

Galerie Klute
Franziskanerplatz, 6 (C3)
U-Bahn Stephansplatz
☎ **513 53 22**
Open Mon.-Fri. 11am-6pm, Sat. 10am-noon.

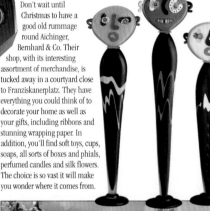

Mozart World Vienna
Kärntnerstrasse, 19 (B3)
U-Bahn Stephansplatz
☎ **514 31 0**
Open Mon.-Fri. 9.30am-7pm, Sat. 9.30am-5pm.

On the ground floor of Steffl there's a shop devoted entirely to Mozart. Hundreds of 'Wolfgangophiles' will delight in the CDs, but you will also enjoy the notebooks, ties decorated with semiquavers, T-shirts bearing pictures of arch-rival Salieri, sweatshirts and children's clothes sporting the Mozart logo. Most delicious of all are the Mozart chocolates (Mozartkugeln) in their unmistakable red and gold packaging.

Galerie Klute is a pretty shop nestling in a courtyard, entirely devoted to crystal and glassware. Some of the items are humorous in design, others more poetic, such as the work of H W Hundstorfer, a master glassmaker whose studio is in the Bohemian forest. His totem poles in molten glass cost ATS3,500-30,000. Don't miss the heads sculpted in glass by the Italian Stefano Toso, the jewellery made by the Slovak Andrej Jakab and the Danish-designed 'Baltic Seaglasses', which cost around ATS1,000 a pair.

Hummel

Lerchenfelder Strasse, 17 (not on map)
U-Bahn Lerchenfelder Strasse
☎ 522 62 63
Open Mon.-Fri. 10am-6pm, Sat. 9am-1pm.

Hummel is heaven for lovers of wooden objects. The shop is on three floors, and each one is a treasure trove full of wooden fruit, flowers, animals, dishes and boxes. Designed by Beate Hummel, all the items on sale are the work of expert craftsmen. You'll love the attractive range of wooden apples (ATS85), sea-lions (ATS110) and hedgehogs sculpted from an exotic wood similar to lime. It's a wonderful shop full of great gift ideas.

Alt-Österreich

Himmelpfortgasse, 7 (C3)
U-Bahn Stephansplatz
☎ 513 48 70
Open Mon.-Fri. 10am-5.30pm.

This Ali Baba's cave, which looks like a cross between a lost property office and a warehouse for secondhand goods, is a like supermarket for the Austro-Hungarian empire. If you manage to get on the right side of the owner, whose moods can be very varied, the slight detour is well worth the effort. You'll find yellowing publicity material, old cufflinks, postcards, theatre tickets, military medals, photographs of opera singers, medals of the imperial family,

and 78 recordings of Herbert von Karajan – all unique testimonies to a past age that make wonderful presents.

Boudoir

Berggasse, 14 (not on map)
U-Bahn Schottentor
☎ 319 10 79
Open Tue.-Fri. 10am-6.30pm, Sat. 10am-1pm.

It may be destiny or just a coincidence that Renate Christian opened Boudoir just a stone's throw from Sigmund Freud's room. The shop sells pretty cushions (ATS349), pillows, curtains and drapes with a pattern featuring a winged phallus and other erotic designs almost worthy of the Marquis de Sade. The young designer trained by Castelbajac and Westwood uses the same libertine designs on a whole range of gifts, including napkins, dressing gowns, and silk negligés that she's christened 'Garbo', 'Colette', 'George Sand' and 'Oscar Wilde'. Frivolous but tasteful!

DELICATESSENS

For those of you wanting to buy delicious food and drink for a picnic at Schönbrunn or to pop into your suitcase to take home with you, Vienna has a selection of quality delicatessens. We've chosen some of the best ones for you to try, where you're guaranteed to find some delicious local specialities. The Viennese are very skilled at packaging and presenting their wares and have a talent for making the most simple things pleasing, as you'll discover.

Schönbichler & Co
Wollzeile, 4 (C2)
U-Bahn Stephansplatz
☎ 512 18 16
Open Mon.-Fri. 10am-6pm,
Sat. 10am-5pm.

This renowned shop, whose doors first opened in 1870, has a wonderful selection of more than a hundred teas. Its shelves are also crammed with luxury jams, quail pâté with morels and Swiss brandies with raspberries or celery (ATS760-870). Tea aficionados come here to stock up on their favourite brew.

Wild
Neuer Markt, 10-11 (B3)
U-Bahn Stephansplatz
☎ 512 53 03
Open Mon.-Fri. 9am-7pm,
Sat. 10am-3pm.

This is a very smart deli, selling a huge range of cheeses and cooked meats. There's a stand-up buffet,

where you can enjoy a crisp mixed salad or delicious open sandwich with chicken on a bed of radicchio. The locals come here for their goulash, pâté de foie gras and *Selch-Kas,* a tasty Styrian cheese. The Wild brothers are happy to deliver to your home, whether it's in Vienna or another country. Pop in for a snack and feast your eyes on the tempting array of fine produce.

Kecks
Herrengasse, 15 (Z2)
U-Bahn Herrengasse
☎ 533 63 67
Open Mon.-Fri. 10am-6pm,
Sat. 10am-3pm.

You can come here to buy smoked ham from Schwarzatal, honey from Styria, horseradish mustard and unusual jams from Waitzendorf. Hearing the evocative names of these places may well tempt you to venture into the Austrian countryside, but you only

have to pop into this deli, located behind the Palais Ferstel, to sample a wide range of delicious Austrian specialities. Kecks carefully selects the farms and dairies that supply it with the best natural produce. Try their stewed apples (ATS34), regional cheeses and the bread made with ten fruits from Mariazell (ATS75). Everything is beautifully wrapped and house specialities are presented in a pretty basket or box.

Arthur Grimm
Kurrentgasse, 10 (B2)
U-Bahn Herrengasse
☎ 533 13 84

Andreas makes wonderful bread at this bakery, using only natural products. The wide range of different breads includes the *Rauchfangkehrer* and *Finnenbrot* (ATS28-41). You can buy pastries and even enjoy a coffee here, too. The prices are very reasonable and it's a lovely spot to relax for a moment.

If you don't have time to go from one deli to another, you should head for the 1st district, where there are two excellent self-service shops with a wide range of produce, **Billa Corso**, Ringstrassen-Galerien (not on map), tel 512 66 25, and **Julius Meinl**, Graben, 19 (B2), ☎ 533 45 86. Both shops are open Mon.-Fri. 10am-7pm, Sat. 10am-5pm.

Even those on the strictest diet will crumble at the sight of the tiny chocolates, which literally melt in your mouth. Their mandarin truffles (ATS11 each) are exquisite and their nougat 'angels' make your head spin!

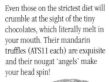

and salmon *tramezzini* (ATS16-19) are amongst the best in the world, or at least in Central Europe! . There are some very good wines too. Self-service meals here cost less but are just as good.

Altmann & Kühne

Graben, 30 (B2)
U-Bahn Stephansplatz
☎ 533 09 27
Open Mon.-Fri. 9am-6.30pm, Sat. 10am-5pm.

Everyone knows A & K, makers of the most delicious chocolates and creative sweets in Vienna, which are always beautifully wrapped.

Zum schwarzen Kameel

Bognergasse, 5 (B2)
U-Bahn Herrengasse
☎ 533 81 25
Open Mon.-Fri. 9am-7pm, Sat. 9am-2.30pm.

'The Black Camel' is a Viennese institution founded in 1618. It isn't simply a restaurant serving delightful local dishes from noon to 3pm, but also a delicatessen where you can do your gourmet shopping in a hushed atmosphere. The vinegars here are famous, as is the Gmund bread stuffed with raisins, rum and nuts, according to a very old recipe (ATS65). Those keen on canapés say that the curry

Eulennest

Himmelpfortgasse, 13 (C3)
U-Bahn Stephansplatz
☎ 513 53 11
Open Mon.-Fri. 1-9pm, Sat. 11am-5pm.

On the ground floor of the Palais Fürstenberg, there's a wine shop run by Susanna Honsowitz. Choose from a delightful selection of 80 red wines and 160 white wines from Austria, together with a wide range of tempting local brandies in a variety of flavours. There's something for everyone here, including exceptional vintage wines, and apricot (*Jesche*) and pear liqueurs (*Altsteirische Winterbirne*) at ATS290. Eulennest is a lovely shop for browsing.

SECONDHAND CLOTHES

You'll only find a handful of secondhand clothes shops in the 1st district. If you're desperate to buy one of last season's outfits, you should head for the traditional flea market (*Flohmarkt*) for a good range of cut-price clothing and accessories. Make sure you bargain, be careful of offers that seem too good to be true (*günstig*) and look out for imitations that may be tempting in price but are disappointing in quality. Even if you don't buy anything, you'll have fun rummaging around.

Women's fashion

Sterngasse, 2 (C1/2)
U-Bahn Stephansplatz
☎ 533 71 30
Open Mon.-Fri. 10am-6pm,
Sat. 10am-4pm.

Herr Hirsch buys factory returns and last season's fashions, and had the idea of opening an outlet for women on the edge of the 'Bermuda Triangle'. His mission is to provide clothes that are high on comfort and quality but low on price, and it's a good place to shop for Italian, Spanish and German jumpers (ATS39), trousers (ATS90) and jackets (ATS890). Here you'll find international labels at very affordable prices.

Gigi

Zedlitzgasse, 11 (C3)
U-Bahn Stubentor
☎ 513 04 95
Open Mon.-Fri. 10am-6pm,
Sat. 10am-5pm.

Gigi is one of the few shops in Vienna whose stock is secondhand but exclusively upmarket. You'll find elegant clothes worn by the smartest Viennese women from the 1st district (probably no more than once or twice) to a concert at the Musikverein or a first night at the Opera. Outfits by Armani, Escada, Mondi and Montana are available at unbeatable prices. Where else would you be able to buy a Westwood jacket for ATS2,800?

First Fashion

Krugerstrasse, 10 (B3)
☎ 513 54 84
U-Bahn Stephansplatz
Open Mon.-Fri. 10am-6pm,
Sat. 10am-5pm.

First Fashion also has big labels at smallish prices (ATS3,800-8,000). Yves Saint Laurent and Sonia Rykiel clothes are often found here, together with a large selection of coats and furs in perfect condition. There's something for everyone at this shop, from formal outfits for important dinners to more risqué dresses for a night on the town. Enjoy a good browse – it's a smart place to shop.

Flea Market

Every Saturday there's a flea market (*Flohmarkt*) in the extension of the Naschmarkt, west of the Kettenbrückengasse U-Bahn station. The stalls are run by a combination of Balkan vendors and local secondhand goods dealers, who sometimes come to blows. There are piles of clothes, old postcards, stamps and ski boots, but the early birds get the best deals, so try to arrive between 8 and 10am or you may miss out on the best bargains.

Jil & Giorgio

Viriotgasse, 6
(not on map)
U-Bahn
Nussdorferstrasse
☎ 319 55 71
Open Mon. 2-6pm, Tue.-Fri.
10am-6pm, Sat. by
appointment.

This shop is not as central as the others but is rather more personal and private, with a smaller collection of women's clothes. You'll find Versace, Armani,

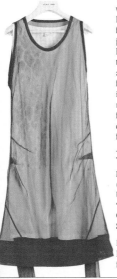

Yamamoto, Dior and even Helmut Lang seconds, sold at a 30% discount. If you don't find what you want here, there's a shop called Hang on a Second only three blocks down at Nussdorferstrasse, 39, where Dvorak & Dworak sell ball gowns for ATS1,690 and Chevignon trousers for ATS1,200.

Kamikaz

Neubaugasse, 55
(not on map)
U-Bahn Neubaugasse
Open Mon.-Wed. 10am-7pm,
Sat. 10am-5pm.

This is the only shop in Vienna with a mix of secondhand and last season's clothes. Come here for your Levi 501 jeans, 1970s jumpers, Hawaiian shirts and little black cocktail dresses. All the clothes come from Paris and are sold at excellent prices by the friendly owner Laurent. The shop isn't much bigger than a fitting room but has hats, glasses and feather boas, as well as a lovely collection of dresses. It's a real find for bargain hunters.

Young Designers

Lindengasse, 39
(not on map)
U-Bahn Neubaugasse
☎ 524 92 32
Open Mon.-Fri. noon-7pm,
Sat. 11am-5pm.

Known locally as YD, Young Designers buys its stock from factories in Vienna, Italy and

England. It has the latest 'streetwear', ends of lines and last season's clothes, all at great reductions. Come here for cool, relaxed clothes for teenagers. A basic T-shirt will cost you ATS70, and you can buy good value shoes, PVC tops and linen jackets by Alles Hanf for ATS500 instead of ATS1,100. It's a very popular place, full of young, trendy locals.

Caritas

Steinheilgasse, 3
(not on map)
U-Bahn Floridsdorf
☎ 259 99 69/ 259 85 77
Open Mon.-
Fri. 9am-
6pm, Sat.
9am-1pm.

Last but not least, there's Caritas, which is quite a long way from the centre but it's only a ten-minute walk from the Floridsdorf station along Leopoldauer Strasse. It's certainly worth making the journey, as it sells not only clothes but also an interesting selection of crockery, furniture, lampshades, carpets and mirrors. It's become quite the fashion in Vienna to come hunting for excellent bargains here.

Practicalities

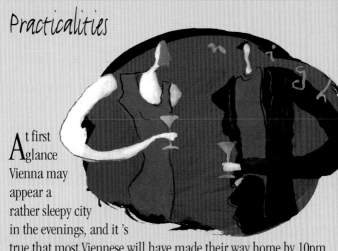

At first glance Vienna may appear a rather sleepy city in the evenings, and it's true that most Viennese will have made their way home by 10pm, unless they're at a classical concert or Strauss festival. However, with the help of our selection of bars and venues, you should be able to find some interesting nightlife. The Bermuda Triangle may be quiet during the day, but at night it comes alive and you can hardly move for fellow revellers.

WHERE IT ALL HAPPENS

The 1st district has many palaces and churches, in which a wide variety of excellent concerts take place, ranging from masses by Mozart and Beethoven, to cello duets and performances by soloists in traditional or historical costume. You'll be able to choose between the Schottenkirche, Palais Pállfy, Palais Lobkowitz, Minoritenkirche and Augustinerkirche. The Opera, Theater an der Wien and Volkstheater are all dotted round the Ring and are easily reached on foot or by train from the centre. The same goes for the trendy bars in the City, which all located round Kärntnerstrasse, Gonzagagasse and Mahlerstrasse. The famous Bermuda Triangle (*Bermuda Dreieck*) at the heart of medieval Vienna, isn't what it once was, but it still has lively spots, such as Krah-Krah and Jazzland. Vienna's clubs are mostly in the 3rd and 8th district, but differentiating between a bar and a club can be difficult in this city.

FINDING OUT WHAT'S ON

If you pick up a national daily newspaper, such as *Die Presse*, there's usually a 'weekend supplement' which has information on theatre and cinema programmes, as well as practical information on various shows. The excellent weekly listings tabloid *Falter* (ATS23) has information on all events (in German), and the free magazine *Wienside* is published every Thursday. It has 32 pages of information on films, concerts (marked with an 'E' for classical and 'U' for contemporary), exhibitions, new plays, the latest ballets and sporting events. Those who want to go to nightclubs can find out where and when on the net (www.club@szenepartynews).

The tourist board publishes a free monthly listings booklet *Programm*, with all you need to know about events at the major opera and concert houses and theatres. It also has a useful guide to concerts, a ball calendar and information on current art exhibitions.

THE DRESS CODE

The majority of Viennese dress up to go to a first night at the opera, Burgtheater or Musikverein (the number one concert hall in Vienna), though you won't be reprimanded for not wearing a tie or evening dress (except by a few grumpy restaurant owners). On the whole the dress code isn't particularly strict, even in the clubs. You can wear whatever you want when you go dancing, but are advised to avoid stilettos, as many of the pavements in the old part of town are a little uneven and high heels can be dangerous.

SAFETY

Some people have tried to compare Vienna with Chicago for its incidence of crime, especially since the fall of the Iron Curtain. However, it's nonsense to do so and you should be fairly safe in the 1st district. The odd pickpocket may operate along Kärntnerstrasse, around Karlsplatz station and on the edges of the Südbahnhof, but all you have to do is behave sensibly and be aware. Don't wear your best jewellery, keep your handbag close to you and a keen eye on your camera or video. Leave your passport in the hotel, don't wander around between the

Westbahnhof and the Volksoper (the so-called 'Gürtel') late at night and avoid the Mexikoplatz in the 2nd district after hours.

TICKETS

The cheapest way of buying a ticket for the Staatsoper, Volksoper or Burgtheater is from the venue's own box office or from a central box office, the Bundestheaterkasse. The sale of tickets commences one month before opening, and tickets for shows between 1 and 30 September are sold between 1 and 30 June. You can also make bookings by phone on 514 4 40, or try their website (www.wien.gv.at). If you don't have a ticket, you can take your chances and turn up on the day at the Staatsoper in Herbert-von-Karajan Platz. The box office underneath the arches is open from 10am until one hour before the show starts. It closes at noon on Saturday.

At the Konzerthaus (concert hall) tickets go on sale three weeks before the performances begin. You can call on 712 12 11 (Mon.-Fri. 8am-6.30pm, Sat.-Sun. 9am-1pm, 4-6.30pm) or reserve by ☎ 712 28 72. You can buy tickets direct from the box office at Lothringerstrasse, 20, open Mon.-Fri. 9am-7.30pm, Sat. until 1pm. A ticket for the Konzerthaus entitles you to travel by public transport in Vienna for 2 hours before and up to 6 hours after the start of the concert.

The Volkstheater sells its tickets by phone (☎ 523 27 76) or ☎ (523 35 01) but you can also get hold of them

FESTWOCHEN AND KLANGBOGEN

There are two very important dates in the Viennese cultural calendar. The Festwochen (Vienna Festival) takes place annually, in May or June, and features a programme of top events with international translations, wonderful scenery, foreign troupes and outdoor shows. For information and tickets, ☎ 586 16 76 or 589 22 22, or ☎ on 586 16 76 49. The Klangbogen (Viennese Summer Festival) is also a wonderful treat for music lovers, with 150 concerts taking place throughout the summer at a variety of venues, including the Musikverein, Konzerthaus, Schonbrunn Park, Palais Pallfy, Bosendorfer-Saal and Hofburg. For more information and tickets, ☎ 4000 84 10 or ☎ 4000 99 84 10. Their offices are at 8, Laudongasse, 29.

directly from the box office, open Mon.-Sat. from 10am. Entry to the box office is via Burggasse.

As a last resort, ask the receptionist at your hotel for advice or go to a special ticket agency, such as **Österreich Ticket**, open every day 10am-7pm, ☎ 960 96.

You can access them on the Internet (tickets@carta.co.at or http://ww.carta.co.at)

Another option for buying tickets is to contact the **Start Internationales Ticket Service** on ☎ 319 06 06.

CONCERTS AND OPERAS

Staatsoper

Opernring, 2 (B3)
U-Bahn Karlsplatz
☎ 514 44 29 60
Tickets ATS200-2,300.

This is Vienna's largest opera house and one of the world's top opera stages. Under supermaestro Herbert von Karajan's leadership, the Staatsoper attracted the very best of the divas. It reopened in 1955 with Beethoven's Fidelio, having been closed in 1944 after a production of Wagner's *Götterdämmerung* (Twilight of the Gods). It has an amazing stairway, 1,700 seats, over 500 *Stehplätze* (standing-room tickets) and the operas are sung in the original version with subtitles in German.

Volksoper

Währinger Strasse, 78 (A1)
U-Bahn Volksoper
514 44 33 18
Tickets ATS100-850.

If you don't fancy queuing all night and spending a fortune on a ticket, come to the Volksoper, where tickets are cheaper and the operas generally a little 'lighter'. For the last one hundred years the excellent programme has included operettas, vaudeville and musicals, ranging from Porgy and Bess and My Fair Lady to Mozart, Janácek and Shostakovitch. There are over 100 *Stehplätze* a night.

Wiener Kammeroper

Fleischmarkt, 24 (C2)
U-Bahn Schwedenplatz
☎ 513 60 72
Tickets ATS70-450.

The singers are less prestigious and the decor less luxurious than those of the Volksoper, but there's no shortage of talent at this opera house. It's an intimate venue, and without it the Strauss operettas and Baroque pieces it stages would remain unknown.

Musikverein

Bosendorferstrasse 12,
(not on map)
U-Bahn Karlsplatz
☎ 505 81 90
Performances 7.30pm.

This temple of classical music and home of the prestigious Viennese Philharmonic Orchestra dates back to 1869. Their New Year's Eve concert is broadcast from the larger of the two ornate concert halls, the *Grosser Saal*, which has the best acoustics in the country, while the Brahms-Saal is used mainly for chamber concerts. Both concert halls have wonderfully sumptuous gilded interiors. Try to attend one of the

orchestra's Sunday concerts, which are an institution.

Volkstheater

Neustiftgasse, 1 (not on map)
U-Bahn Volkstheater
☎ 523 27 76
Tickets ATS50-500.

This beautiful theatre opened in 1889 is less exclusive than the Burgtheater. Its plays tend to focus on social themes, by authors such as Dürrenmatt, Goldoni or Nestroy. The latter was writing plays in the Biedermeier era and they're full of comical wordplay, turbulent emotions and the occasional extraordinary volte-face. If you're a German speaker, try to see one of his plays – you'll enjoy it.

Burgtheater

Dr. Karl-Lueger-Ring, 2 (A2)
U-Bahn Herrengasse
☎ 514 44 42 18
Tickets ATS50-500.

Known to its fans simply as the 'Burg', this is one of the best German-speaking theatres. It was built in 1888 and has been under the directorship of the talented Claus Peymann since 1986. The foyer and staircase are stunning, and there's a wonderful fresco by Gustav Klimt. The auditorium had to be renovated after damage during the bombing of 1945. The programme itself concentrates on serious drama and has been quite controversial. On the opening night of a play by Thomas Bernhard, some conservative locals deposited manure at the entrance as a statement of their thoughts on the production.

Hofkapelle

Hofburg, Schweizerhof (A2)
U-Bahn Herrengasse
☎ 533 99 27
Performance every day at 9.15am (exc. July & Aug.)
Tickets ATS60-340.

This is where the famous Vienna Boys Choir (*Wiener Sängerknaben*) sing mass every Sunday. Emperor Maximilian I founded this musical institution in 1498, and tickets are usually sold out weeks in advance, though a few are sold on Fridays from 3 to 5pm. You can also hear the choir at the Konzerthaus every Friday at 3.30pm (in May, June, September and October).

Konzerthaus

Lothringerstrasse, 20
(not on map)
U-Bahn Stadtpark
☎ 712 12 11
Performances every day 7.30pm (Sat. 3.30pm & 5pm).

There are three separate, recently renovated, halls in the Konzerthaus – the Grosser Saal, used for orchestral performances, and the Mozartsaal and Schubertsaal, in which chamber music, modern music and Lieder are performed. The building opened in 1913, and wonderful artists have played or sung here, including the pianist Oleg Maisenberg, the organist Jean Guillou, and Cecilia Bartoli in the role of Almirena.

Mozarthaus

Singerstrasse, 7 (C3)
U-Bahn Stephansplatz
☎ 911 90 77
Performances: every day 7.30pm (Sat. 5pm).
Tickets ATS250-450.

In 1781 Mozart, still in the service of Count Colloredo, performed many times in this house, which belonged to the order of the Teutonic Knights. Today internationally-renowned soloists give great performances of music by Mozart (of course), as well as Haydn, Schubert and Beethoven.

BARS

Oblomov

Werdertorgasse, 4 (B1)
☎ 533 88 66
Open every day 7pm-4am.

Oblomov is relatively calm in the early evening, but becomes increasingly busy until reaching fever pitch after midnight, especially on 'cocktail theme' evenings, when a range of vodka, champagne and Cuban specials are the order of the day. But relax, there's no need to speak Russian.

Blaue Bar

Philharmonikerstrasse, 4 (B3)
☎ 51 456 0
Open every day 11pm-2am.

If you don't like noisy bars with neon lighting and throbbing music, then try the bar at the Hotel Sacher. The atmosphere's relaxing, the music's soft and unobtrusive and they serve one of the best cocktails you'll find in Vienna. The 'Anna Sacher' is made with orange juice, apricot liqueur, a dash of grenadine, a little vermouth and more than a drop of champagne. It's absolutely delicious!

La Fuente

Burggasse 23 (not on map)
☎ 524 03 76
Open every day 4pm-4am.

This bar designed by the architect Heinz Lutter is Spanish in style, as its name (meaning 'The Spring') suggests. You can have cocktails, *tapas*, and *ensaladas de naranjas valencianas* (Valencia orange salad) or just enjoy a lovely bottle of Rioja wine. The bar is on four floors, and 'Happy Hour' is from 4pm and 7pm.

Guessclub

**Kaunitzgasse 3
(not on map)**
☎ 585 51 08
Open every day 3pm-2am.

Markus Geiswinkler has come up with a great concept for 'night-surfers' on the Internet, and his multi-media club is the envy of many bar owners. You can surf the web while sipping delicious cocktails with trendy names, such as 'Safe Sex on the Beach', a mixture of rum, vodka, galliano, coconut and orange juice. Choose from 67 pages of cocktail suggestions! Guessclub is on line every day, allowing you to enjoy a browse with your brunch on a Sunday morning.

Planters Club

Zelinkagasse, 4 (B1)
☎ 533 33 93
Open every day 5pm-4am.

Planters Club has palm trees, fans and comfortable chairs, and when you step inside you feel as if you've been transported to the set of 'Out of Africa'. Peter Rossler has created the authentic atmosphere of an Indonesian plantation for your delight, and you can relax while sipping a glass of rum or one of the 350 brands of whisky.

Krah-Krah

Rabensteig, 8 (C1)
☎ 533 81 93
**Open Mon.-Sat. 11am-2am,
Sun. 11am-2am.**

Before you head for a nightclub, drop in at this interesting bar

in the Bermuda Triangle. It has an excellent selection of draught beers, and is always busy, smoky and noisy. There's no air conditioning at Krah-Krah, but there's plenty of rock music. Choose from 55 different brands of beer at ATS35 a glass.

Barfly's

**Esterházygasse, 33
(not on map)
☎ 586 08 25
Open every day
6pm-3am (8pm-3am in summer).**

Barfly is a small but friendly bar that's successfully resisted the latest fads. It serves 150 kinds of rum, 40 brands of tequila and enough cocktails to keep you very happy while relaxing to the music of Frank Sinatra.

Kruger's

**Krugerstrasse,
5 (C3)
☎ 512 24 55
Open every day
5pm-4am.**

This spacious and relaxing American bar is located near the Opera, and is in competition with Planters to a certain extent with a wide choice of cognacs, armagnacs and fine cigars.

First Floor

**Seitenstettengasse,
5 (C1)
☎ 533 78 6
Open Mon.-Sat. 7pm-4am, Sun. 7pm-3am.**

First Floor was renovated by Eichinger and Knechtl in 1994, and is one of the most beautiful bars in Vienna. Once you've ensconced yourself at the bar, you won't want to leave. There's an almost hypnotic aquarium with floating plants, which adds to the cool, relaxing atmosphere. Enjoy excellent cocktails such as 'Manhattan Specials' at ATS95, while listening to the piano and double bass.

Reiss-Bar

**Marco-d'Aviano-Gasse, 1
(not on map)
U-Bahn Stephansplatz
☎ 512 71 98
Open Mon.-Fri. 11am-3am,
Sat. 10am-3am, Sun. 11am-2am.**

This is the only authentic champagne bar in Vienna, and is the favourite haunt of well-heeled forty-somethings tasting champagnes from all over the world (from ATS90 a glass). Enjoy oysters, caviar and Irish salmon with your fizz, but be prepared for a hefty bill for the pleasure. The Reiss-Bar is definitely not the place for those on a budget but it's a memorable place.

NIGHTCLUBBING

U4

**Schönbrunner Strasse, 222
(not on map)
U-Bahn Meidling-
Hauptstrasse
☎ 815 83 07
Open every day 11pm-5am.**

This is the most internationally famous nightclub in Vienna, and a Mecca for alternative, 'underground' clubbers. London DJs come here to entertain fans of house, techno, rock and Indie music. It's a large venue and has a 'Heaven Gay Night' every Thursday. Try to fit in a visit if you have time.

Meierei im Stadtpark

**Am Heumarkt, 2a
(not on map)
☎ 714 61 59 0
Open Thu.-Sat. from 10pm.
Entry charge ATS100.**

If you're itching for a dance, try to be in Vienna on a Thursday so you can enjoy an evening with DJ Samir. His 'groove' nights start at 10pm and he'll keep you on the dance floor into the early hours with his irresistible rhythms. On Fridays the Sunshine group plays alternative Brazilian music.

Volksgarten

**1, Burgring, 1 (A3)
U-Bahn Volkstheater
☎ 533 05 18 0
Open every day 10pm-5am.**

Round off a lovely summer's day in Vienna with dinner at the Volksgarten Pavillon. Hot dishes are served until midnight, and you can dance outdoors until 2am. This is one of Vienna's trendiest clubs, more commercial than Arena (see p. 123) but less frantic than U4 (see left). There's reggae music on Fridays, but if you're in the mood for a waltz, you can go to the nearby Tanz club.

Chez Gerard

**Lederergasse, 11 (not on map)
☎ 402 07 86
Open every day 8pm-4am.**

Arthur Singer (alias King Arthur) was the DJ at Heaven for six years and has an amazing collection of records. He plays music from the 1960s to 1990s on the smallish dance floor. The decor is modest too, and there are two bars with separate seating areas. On Sundays there's a gay and lesbian tea dance from 5pm to 1am. Mario Soldo is in charge of this event, which can get quite wild.

Massive

**Untere Weissbergerstrasse, 27 (not on map)
Open Fri.-Sat. 11pm till late.**

If you're a devoted fan of house music, make your way here and join the locals at this recently opened 'underground' venue. Let's hope it lasts the distance.

Jenseits

**Nelkengasse (not on map)
☎ 57 12 33
Open Mon.-Sat. 10pm-4am.**

Jenseits is a good place to come if you don't like dance factories

such as Fun Factory, which recently opened in Hall 1 of the Leopoldstadt Exhibition Park. It's the smartest and most intimate club in Mariahilf, with a crimson 1950s decor.

Eschenbach Palast

Eschenbachgasse, 11 (not on map)

This is another relatively unknown hot venue. On Friday night the palace is turned into a disco, as if by magic. The paintings are taken down, the furniture is removed and a mobile bar is put in place, in readiness for an evening of salsa in ancient surroundings.

ROCK

Wuk

Währinger Strasse 59 (A1)
☎ 401 21 44
Open every day from 8 or 10pm till late

Wuk is an alternative venue, housed in a former car warehouse. It's been going for over 15 years and is a perfect spot for a torrid

rock concert. It's very post-industrial and the atmosphere revs like an overheated engine. The air-conditioning in the main hall has been renovated, so things do cool down a bit.

Arena

3, Baumgasse, 80 (not on map)
U-Bahn Erdberg
☎ 798 85 95
Open every day from 9pm till late.
Entry charge ATS120-300.

If you can't live without your weekly dose of rock, heavy metal and hardcore music, then take a risk and head for Schartlgasse (U-Bahn Liesing) in search of

an unreliable rave. Alternatively, make your way out to Arena, a former slaughterhouse, where you can enjoy all-night raves and outdoor concerts in June and July. Check the listings before you make the journey, as it's a long way to go to be disappointed.

JAZZ

Jazzland

Franz Josefskai, 29 (C1)
☎ 533 25 75.
Open Tue.-Sat. 7pm-2am (occasionally Sun. & Mon.)

There's a great ambiance in this jazz club, in which excellent bands play four or five times a week, starting at 9pm. It's a very popular venue and probably the best jazz club in Vienna. You'll find it next to the Ruprechtskirche, the city's oldest church. This is the place to come if you're a jazz fan.

Porgy & Bess

Spiegelgasse, 2 (B3)
☎ 512 84 38
Open Mon.-Thu. 7pm-2am, Fri.-Sat. 8pm-4am.
Entry charge ATS170-220.

All sorts of jazz fans come to this venue to enjoy an eclectic programme, embracing such groups as the Dhafer Youssef Ensemble and Doretta Carta and the Funkmonsters. There are session nights on Wednesdays, when entry charges are lower.

More handy words and phrases

Many Austrians speak English, but they'll really appreciate it if you make an effort to speak their language, especially since you cannot assume that they'll all understand English. So here are some handy words and expressions which may prove useful during your stay in Vienna, in addition to those on the back flap of the cover, where you'll also find a guide to pronunciation. You should be aware that Austrians speak German with a distinct accent and that they have their own dialect, but they will generally speak standard German when conversing with foreigners.

USEFUL EXPRESSIONS

I don't speak much German
Ich spreche kaum Deutsch.

What does that mean?
Was bedeutet das?

Can you translate that for me?
Können Sie mir das übersetzen?

Can you write it down for me?
Können Sie es bitte aufschreiben?

Can you help me?
Können Sie mir helfen?

Can I have…?
Kann ich…haben?

Where can I find…?
Wo finde ich…?

I'll take it
Ich nehme es.

No, I don't like it
Nein, das gefällt mir nicht.

What is your name?
Wie heissen Sie?

IN THE RESTAURANT

Mushrooms
Champignons/Pilze

Eggs
Eier

Potatoes
Erdäpfel/Kartoffeln

Vinegar
Essig

Baked
Gebacken

Roasted
Gebraten

Steamed
Gedämpft

Grilled
Gegrillt

Home-made
Hausgemacht

Cabbage
Kohl

Dumplings
Knödel

Pasta
Nockerl/Nudeln

Pancakes
Palatschinken

Red/white wine
Rotwein/Weisswein

Pickled cabbage
Sauerkraut

Whipped cream
Schlagobers

Ham and fried eggs
Spiegeleier mit Schinken

Spinach
Spinat

Veal in breadcrumbs
Wiener Schnitzel

Sausages (see p. 15)
Würste

What would you recommend?
Was würden Sie mir empfehlen?

That was a very good meal
Das Essen war sehr gut, danke.

Where are the toilets?
Wo sind die Toiletten?

I'd like to pay
Ich möchte zahlen

AT THE BANK

Where is the nearest bank?
Wo ist die nächste Bank?

I would like to cash a travellers cheque.
Ich möchte einen Reisecheck einlösen.

I would like to change some pounds/dollars.
Ich möchte Pfund/Dollar wechseln.

I would like to pay in cash.
Ich möchte mit Bargeld bezahlen.

MONEY

Cash dispensing machine
das Geldautomat

Exchange rate (What is the exchange rate?)
der Wechselkurs (Wie ist der Wechselkurs?)

Banknotes
die Banknoten

Coins
die Münzen

Small change (do you have small change?)
das Kleingeld (Haben Sie Kleingeld?)

SIGNS AND NOTICES

Entrance
Eingang

Exit
Ausgang

Emergency exit
Notausgang

No entrance
Kein Zutritt

Arrival
Ankunft

Departure
Abfahrt

Free
Frei

Occupied
Besetzt

Attention/Beware
Achtung!/Vorsicht!

Prohibited
Verboten

Hospital
Krankenhaus

Police
Polizei

Women's toilets
Damen/Frauen

Men's toilets
Herren/Männer

TIME AND PLACE

Monday: Montag
Tuesday: Dienstag
Wednesday: Mittwoch
Thursday: Donnerstag
Friday: Freitag
Saturday: Samstag
Sunday: Sonntag
Today/tomorrow/yesterday:
heute/morgen/gestern
On the right: rechts
On the left: links
Straight ahead: gerade aus

Conversion tables for clothes shopping

Women's sizes

Shirts/dresses

U.K	U.S.A	EUROPE
8	6	36
10	8	38
12	10	40
14	12	42
16	14	44
18	16	46

Sweaters

U.K	U.S.A	EUROPE
8	6	44
10	8	46
12	10	48
14	12	50
16	14	52

Shoes

U.K	U.S.A	EUROPE
3	5	36
4	6	37
5	7	38
6	8	39
7	9	40
8	10	41

Men's sizes

Shirts

U.K	U.S.A	EUROPE
14	14	36
14$\frac{1}{2}$	14$\frac{1}{2}$	37
15	15	38
15$\frac{1}{2}$	15$\frac{1}{2}$	39
16	16	41
16$\frac{1}{2}$	16$\frac{1}{2}$	42
17	17	43
17$\frac{1}{2}$	17$\frac{1}{2}$	44
18	18	46

Suits

U.K	U.S.A	EUROPE
36	36	46
38	38	48
40	40	50
42	42	52
44	44	54
46	46	56

Shoes

U.K	U.S.A	EUROPE
6	8	39
7	9	40
8	10	41
9	10.5	42
10	11	43
11	12	44
12	13	45

More useful conversions

1 centimetre	0.39 inches	1 inch	2.54 centimetres
1 metre	1.09 yards	1 yard	0.91 metres
1 kilometre	0.62 miles	1 mile	1. 61 kilometres
1 litre	1.76 pints	1 pint	0.57 litres
1 gram	0.35 ounces	1 ounce	28.35 grams
1 kilogram	2.2 pounds	1 pound	0.45 kilograms

This guide was written by **Reto Morgenthaler**, who would like
to thank **Veronika Beiweis, Laurent Candelon, Jean-Philippe Follet,
Michael Hirsch, Beate Hummel, Aniko Kiss-Marcovic, Herr & Frau
Klute, Ingeborg Millet, Tamas Pozsgai** and **Roland Zimmermann**.
Contributions were also made by **Marie Barbelet** and **Aurelie Jones**.
Translated by **Jane Moseley**
Design English edition **Vanessa Byrne**
Project manager and copy editor **Margaret Rocques**
Series editor **Liz Coghill**
Additional research and assistance: **Vanessa Dowell, Jeremy Smith**
and **Christine Bell**

We have done our best to ensure the accuracy of the information contained in this guide.
However, addresses, phone numbers, opening times etc. inevitably do change from time
to time, so if you find a discrepancy please do let us know. You can contact us at:
hachetteuk@orionbooks.co.uk or write to us at Hachette UK, address below.

Hachette UK guides provide independent advice. The authors and compilers do not accept any
remuneration for the inclusion of any addresses in these guides.

Please note that we cannot accept any responsibility for any loss, injury or inconvenience
sustained by anyone as a result of any information or advice contained in this guide.

Photograph acknowledgements

Inside pages:
All photographs were taken by **Nicolas EDWIGE**, with the exception of the following:
Pawel Wysocki, Hémisphères: p.30 (b.l.). **Hachette**: p. 21 (b.l.), p.22 (c.l.), p.23 (c.l.), p.28 (b.l.), p.32 (c.c.), p.34
(c.l.;c.r.), p.35 (c.r.). **Wiener Porzellanmanufaktur Augarten/Elwood**: p.12 (t.r.), p.101 (c.r.). **Woka**: p.13 (t.l.),
p.100 (c.l.). **Sankt Urban, Thomas Apolt**: p.47 (b.l.). **Hummel**: p.65 (b.l.), p.110 (t.r.), p.111 (c.l.). **Konig von
Ungarn**: p.70 (t.l.). **Sacher**: p.71 (b.l.), p.79 (c.c.). **Ana Grand Hotel**: p.73 (t.l.). **Am Schubertring**: p.73 (b.r.).
Unkai Teppan Yaki: p.77 (t.l.). **Modus Vivendi**: p.85 (t.l.) (b.l.). **Misfit, Anthony Gryton**: p.88 (c.r.). **Hartmann**:
p.90 (t.r.). **Michaela E. Lange**: p.91 (t.l.). **Schullin & Seitner**: p.91 (c.c.), p.92 (t.r.) p. 93 (t.l.). **Adil Besim**: p.106
(c.l.). **Prachner**: p.109 (t.l.). **H.W. Hundstorfer, Galerie Klute**: p.110 (c.r.). **Boudoir**: p.111 (t.r.). **Guess Club**:
p.120 (b.r.).

Front cover
Nicholas Edwige, except for **Stock Image/Pacific Productions**: t.c.; **Image Bank/W. Bokelberg**: b.c.; **Fotogram
Stones/Lee Page**: c.r.

Back cover
Nicolas Edwige

Illustrations: Monique Prudent

Cartography: © Hachette Tourisme

If you're staying on for a few days and would like to try some new places, the next pages give you a wide choice of hotels, restaurants and bars, listed by district and with addresses.

Although you can just turn up at a restaurant and have a meal (except in the most prestigious establishments), don't forget to book your hotel several days in advance (see page 68).

Enjoy your stay!

STAYING ON
A LITTLE LONGER

Cathedral

Domizil
Schulerstrasse, 14
☎ 513 31 99
☎ 512 34 84
U-Bahn Stephansplatz
Email domizil@gmx.net
Double room ATS1,300-1,500.
This pension has 40 adequately furnished but quite small rooms that are clean but a little clinical in their decor. However, it's in a good strategic location, the staff are friendly and the breakfasts are excellent.

Graben
Dorotheergasse, 23
☎ 470 42 72 0
☎ 470 42 72 14
graben@kremslehner.hotels.or.at
U-Bahn Stephansplatz
Double room ATS1,600-1,950.
This hotel has a great location, and is a pleasant place to stay, with smart, though rather dark rooms.

Amadeus
Wildpretmarkt, 5
☎ 533 87 38
☎ 533 87 38 38
U-Bahn Stephansplatz
Double room ATS1,950-2,000.
There are 30 smart rooms in this hotel with a modern façade. It's situated in the small street connecting Brandstätte with Landskrongasse, and has red carpets, chandeliers and elegant upholstered furniture. However, Amadeus is closed during the Christmas holidays.

Fleischmarkt

Pension Christina
Hafnersteig, 7
☎ 533 29 61
☎ 533 29 61 11
U-Bahn Schwedenplatz
Double room ATS1,020-1,400.
Don't be put off by the rather daunting façade of this 3-star pension, a stone's throw from the Greek Orthodox Church (Griechische Kirche). The staff are welcoming and friendly, and the 33 rooms are pleasant and relatively quiet. It's centrally located.

Hotel Austria
Fleischmarkt, 20
☎ 515 23
☎ 515 23 506
Email hotelaus@eunet.at
U-Bahn Schwedenplatz
Double room ATS1,365-1,770.
This is a small 3-star hotel with 46 rooms situated in a cul-de-sac (Wolfengasse). The rooms are quiet and nicely furnished, breakfast is eaten round a fountain and prices are quite reasonable.

Mercure Wien Zentrum
Fleischmarkt, 1
☎ 513 12 74
☎ 513 12 74 15
U-Bahn Schwedenplatz
Double room ATS1,780-1,980.
Location, location, location! You couldn't hope for anywhere more central than this new hotel which caters for fewer organised groups than its sister hotel, the Mercure Pannonia. It's a hop and a skip from the synagogue and the Stephansdom Cathedral.

Karlsplatz/Wieden

Hotel Zur Wiener Staatsoper
Krugerstrasse, 11
☎ 513 12 74
☎ 513 12 74 15
Email Staatsoper@hotels.or.at
U-Bahn Karlsplatz
Double room ATS1,200-1,700.
This 3-star hotel has a lovely 19th-century façade and is located close to the Staatsoper and Albertina. It has 22 quiet rooms.

Pension Am Operneck
Karntnerstrasse, 47
☎ 512 93 10
U-Bahn Karlsplatz
Double room ATS900.
This small pension has 7 simple, functional and clean rooms, in which breakfast is served. Opera-goers will love its position, as they can join the queue at dawn by just stepping out of the door.

Das Triest
4, Wiedner Haupstrasse, 12
☎ 589 18 0
☎ 589 18 18
U-Bahn Karlsplatz
Double room ATS2800.
Sir Terence Conran redesigned this former coaching inn on the Vienna to Trieste road. The rooms are all en suite and very pretty. There's a courtyard garden and a good restaurant called the Collio.

Erzherhog Rainer
Wiedner Haupstrasse, 27-29
☎ 501 11 0
☎ 501 11 350
U-Bahn Karlsplatz
Double room ATS1,460-2,360.
This hotel, founded in 1913, was home to Russian officers after World War II. The rooms have been modernised, and the hotel offers a friendly, efficient service.

Westbahnhof

Mercure Pannonia
Matrosengasse, 6-8
☎ 599 010
☎ 597 69 00
U-Bahn Westbahnhof
Double room ATS1,530-1,780.
There are 210 comfortable and functional rooms in this hotel, close to the Westbahnhof and the Mariahilf district. The service is friendly, and the self-service buffet breakfast excellent.

Arcotel Wimberger
Neubaugürtel, 34-36
☎ 521 65 0
☎ 521 65 810
U-Bahn Westbahnhof
Double room ATS1,600-2,250.
This is a very modern establishment a stone's throw from the Westbahnhof, equipped with a sauna, fitness centre, solarium and garage, plus 225 rooms with mini-bars, safes, hair-dryers and special adaptors for computers.

Josephstadt/Neubau

Wild
Lange Gasse, 10
☎ 406 51 74
☎ 402 21 68
U-Bahn Lerchenfelder Strasse
Double room ATS590.
This small pension has 21 rooms with shared facilities, and is a favourite haunt of backpackers. It's in a student area, a short walk from the Ring, and the owners are very friendly, and the prices are extremely reasonable. You should book well ahead.

Jugendherberge

Mythengasse, 7
☎ 523 63 16/523 74 62
Bus 48A or
U-Bahn Volkstheater
Bed ATS140.
This is the most central of the official hostels and a good place for those on a tight budget – you can eat here for ATS60. There's an annex at Neustiftgasse, 85 (just round the corner), and there are 243 dorm beds. Book ahead.

Alla Lenz

Halbgasse, 3-5
☎ 523 69 89
🅕 523 69 89 55
U-Bahn Burggasse
Double room ATS680-1,380.
This 4-star pension has 23 rooms, each with shower, cable TV, telephone and air-conditioning. There's even a swimming pool on the roof, a café and a garage nearby.

Museum

Museumstrasse, 3
☎ 523 44 26
🅕 523 44 26 30
U-Bahn Volkstheater
Double room ATS1,250-1,690.
Another 4-star pension, located above a cinema in a late 19th-century building near the museum district. Several rooms are very large, but the decor is a little antiquated in some of them.

Stubentor

Radisson SAS

Weihburggasse, 32
Parkring 16
☎ 51 51 70
🅕 51 22 216
U-Bahn Stubentor
Double room ATS3,460-4,500
This former Ringstrasse palace is now a luxury hotel with 246 rooms. Expensive, but the service is excellent and it has a very good restaurant, La Siècle im Ersten.

Other districts

Regina

Rooseveltplatz, 15
☎ 40 44 60
🅕 40 88 39 20
reservation@kremlehner.hotels.or.at
U-Bahn Schottentor
Double room ATS1,600-1,950

This is another Ringstrasse hotel, dating back to 1896, with heavy Viennese decor in the foyer and some of the rooms. It's a ten-minute walk to the 1st district, and there's a lovely dining room. However, it's sometimes invaded by hordes of tourists, so beware.

Ananas

Rechte Wienzeile, 93-95
☎ 546 20 0
🅕 545 42 42
U-Bahn Pilgrimgasse
Double room ATS1,680-2,300.
This modern hotel has 533 rooms, all hidden behind a Jugendstil façade. It's in a perfect strategic location for exploring the 5th (Margareten) and 6th (Mariahilf) districts, and is on the Karlsplatz/ Schönbrunn U-Bahn line.

Arkadenhof

Viriotgasse, 5
☎ 310 08 37
🅕 310 76 86
U-Bahn Nussdorferstrasse
Double room ATS1,580-1,880.
This hotel opened in 1992 in a district that has little to recommend it except for its proximity to the vineyards of Grinzing and Seivering. It has 45 comfortable rooms.

Schloss Wilhelminenberg

Savoyenstrasse, 2
☎ 48 58 50 30
🅕 485 48 76
whbg@wigast.com
Bus 46B or
U-Bahn Ottakring
Double room ATS1,310-1,620.
This lovely castle on the edge of the Vienna Woods has been converted into a 3-star hotel with 87 rooms. It has a wonderful view over Vienna.

Thuringer Hof

Jorgerstrasse, 4-8
☎ 401 79 0
🅕 401 79 600
U-Bahn Alser Strasse
Double room ATS1,120-2,160.
There are 80 rooms in this hotel, some of them very spacious. There's a roof terrace and parking, but the hotel is closed during the Christmas holidays.

Cathedral

Walter Bauer
Sonnenfelsgasse, 17
☎ 512 98 71
U-Bahn Stephansplatz
Open Tue.-Fri., noon-2pm, 6-11pm,
Sat. 6-11pm.
Discerning gourmets and romantic diners are served top quality food at this establishment. The menu is expensive (ATS300-500) but tempting, and the service impeccable. Try the polenta in pumpkin oil.

Neu Wien
Bäckerstrasse, 5
☎ 513 06 66
U-Bahn Stephansplatz
Open every day 6pm-midnight.
The restaurant is in a vaulted room that can get rather smoky by the end of the night. It's a favourite haunt of artists and gallery owners, and the food tends to be elaborate. The price ranges between ATS90 and ATS200 per dish.

Do & Do
Stephansplatz, 12
☎ 535 39 69
U-Bahn Stephansplatz
Open Mon.-Sat. noon – 3pm, 6-11pm.
Do & Do is on the seventh floor of the Hass-Haus, and is a very trendy place to eat. It's not an intimate or particularly atmospheric spot, but the view over the Stephansdom is wonderful. Shellfish are a speciality, and there are also Thai soups, sushi and Tuscan vegetables. Prices start at ATS175.

Zum finsteren Stern
Sterngasse, 2
☎ 535 81 52
U-Bahn Schwedenplatz
Open Mon.-Sat. 1-11pm.
In this tiny wine bar you can eat house ragout for ATS100, or nibble on a mixed salad. However, it's the chef who decides what you eat, according to his mood and market availability on the day.

Rosenberger Markt
Maysedergasse, 2
☎ 512 34 58
U-Bahn Stephansplatz
Open every day 11am-11pm.
This self-service basement restaurant has a buffet with a large choice of salads at ATS29 a plate. You can also have hot dishes and pastries. Eat your fill for under ATS100!

Augustiner-Keller
Augustinerstrasse, 1
☎ 533 10 26
U-Bahn Stephansplatz
Open every day 11am-11pm.
Just behind the Opera, this cellar houses a restaurant with communal tables, serving wine from an Augustinian convent and an assortment of meats and cheeses. Both locals and tourists eat here, and the best time to come is after 6.30pm.

Freyung

Bei Max
Landhausgasse, 2
☎ 533 73 59
U-Bahn Herrengasse
Open Mon.-Fri. 11am-10pm.
The service at Max's Place can be a bit slow, but the house specialities, mostly Carinthian in flavour, come in very generous portions that are certainly worth the wait. Prices range from ATS100 to ATS200 a dish.

Stubenviertel

Englander
1, Postgasse, 2
☎ 512 27 34
U-Bahn Stubentor
Open every day 11.30am-11.30pm.
This is a pleasant Kaffeehaus frequented by journalists and young trendies. It's not far from the MAK, and you can enjoy a cup of coffee or piping hot dish of Tafelspitz (boiled beef). The lunch menu costs ATS100.

Naschmarkt/Belvedere

Stern
Gumpendorferstrasse, 34
☎ 586 92 20
U-Bahn Kettenbruckengasse
Open every day 6pm-midnight
This mini-restaurant on two floors is a stone's throw from the Café Sperl. It's trendy without being pretentious and serves Austrian and Italian dishes, with chocolate mousse to follow. All this costs just ATS100-200.

Artner
Floragasse, 6
(corner of Neumanngasse)
☎ 503 50 33
U-Bahn Taubstummengasse
Open Mon.-Fri. 11am-1am, Sat.-Sun. 6pm-midnight.
Enjoy Mediterranean cuisine at this restaurant, prepared in his own unique way by a young chef from Lower Austria. Carpaccio, lamb cutlets with rosemary and homemade ewe's cheese are all on the menu.

Green Cottage
Kettenbrückengasse, 3
☎ 586 65 81
U-Bahn Kettenbrückengasse
Open Mon.-Sat. noon-2pm, 6-11pm.
This is the best Chinese restaurant in Vienna, where you should try the Yuxiang-style crunchy meatballs and desserts made with red bean and sweet chestnut purée.

Josephstadt/Uni

Dennstedt
Laudongasse, 36
☎ 403 83 24
U-Bahn Rathaus
Open every day 6pm-midnight.
The food is less interesting than the customers in this restaurant, where you'll spot models and show biz types. The wine list is impressive, however, as is the tagliatelle with capers.

Fish & Orange
Ebendorferstrasse, 10
☎ 408 70 71
U-Bahn Rathaus
Open Mon.-Fri. 11.30am-midnight,
Sat. 7pm-midnight.
This glass and marble bar is situated below the university, and its walls are decorated with love poems. Try the risotto or fish kebabs, and enjoy a very reasonably-priced lunch for ATS100.

Landstrasse

El Fontroussi
Reisnerstrasse 39
☎ 712 54 30
U-Bahn Stadtpark
Open Mon.-Fri. 11.30am-2.30pm, 6-11pm,
Sat. 6-11pm.
Fish and poultry dishes with excellent sauces are served here in wood-panelled surroundings at very reasonable prices (ATS90-220 a dish). Booking is advisable as it gets pretty busy.

Max
Posthorngasse, 6
☎ 713 34 49
U-Bahn Rochusgasse
This little-known restaurant in a street overlooking the Ungargasse, is a favourite with artists and designers. Traditional dishes are served at modest prices, and you can admire Max's own paintings on the walls.

Alsergrund

Bordeaux
Servitengasse, 2
☎ 315 63 63
U-Bahn Schottenring
Open Mon.-Sat. 6pm-midnight.
A 3-minute walk from the Freud Museum, you can sample delicious French dishes and wines at Bordeaux (the restaurant!). Prices are reasonable (from ATS175), and the menu includes foie gras and Cointreau mousse.

Stein's Diner
Kolingasse, 1
☎ 310 95 15
U-Bahn Schottentor
Open Mon.-Sat. 7pm-1am.
Stein's Diner looks American, the dishes have an Italian and Asian influence and there's a designer clientèle. It's attached to the Café Stein (see p.63), and the evening menu (ATS140) includes tasty basmati rice dishes with ginger and vitello tonnato. Trendy music, on-line facilities and vegetarian options make this a popular spot.

Spittelberg/Neubau

Lux
7, Spittelberggasse, 3
☎ 526 94 91
U-Bahn Volkstheater
Open every day noon-3pm, 6pm-midnight.
Lux is a café, bar and restaurant, that can get rather chaotic at times. However, it's a great place to come for a quick lunch, and the emphasis is on healthy dishes, including vegetarian options and pizzas. Both food and atmosphere are good.

Pontini
Burggasse, 103
(entrance via Halbgasse)
☎ 522 38 15
U-Bahn Burggasse
Open Mon.-Sat. noon-2pm, 6-11pm.
The decor at Pontinis is 1920s style, tastefully renovated, and the food is traditional. Enjoy goulash, schnitzels and other hearty fare in this pleasant Beisl (a Viennese version of a pub, usually with wood-panelling and shared tables).

Other districts

Vikerls
Wurffelgasse, 4
☎ 894 34 30
U-Bahn Gumpendorfer Strasse
Open Tue.-Sun. 11am-2.30pm, 6-11pm.
Vikerls is one of the few attractive venues near the Westbahnhof, and serves fresh produce, good wines and excellent meat dishes in wood-panelled surroundings. The evening menu costs ATS400.

Mraz & Sohn
Wallensteinstrasse, 59
☎ 330 45 94
Tram 5
Open Mon.-Fri., 11am-2.30pm, 6-10.30pm.
This restaurant is expensive (ATS700-1,000 for a meal), but the cuisine is very imaginative and includes such dishes as 'Tandoori seafood with asparagus'. It's a shame the surrounding area is a little sinister.

Am Reisenberg
Oberer Reisenbergweg, 15
☎ 320 93 93
Bus 38A
Open Wed.-Mon. 4-11pm.
This Heuriger in the village of Grinzing is famous for its cooked meats, soufflés (ATS40) and plum tarts. There's a lovely view from the terrace.

RESTAURANTS

Cathedral

Diglas
1, Wollzeile, 10
☎ 512 57 65
U-Bahn Stephansplatz
Open Mon.-Wed. 7am-
11.30pm, Thu.-Sat. 7am-
1pm,
Sun. 8am-11.30pm.
*Diglas opened in 1923 and was
the favourite haunt of Franz Lehar
(composer of The Merry Widow).
It was reopened as a café in the
1990s by the original owner's
grandson. It's a rather smoky
Kaffeehaus, serving tasty pastries
in a warm, welcoming atmosphere. In summer, you can sit outside.*

Korb
1, Brandstatte, 9
☎ 533 72 15
U-Bahn Stephansplatz
Open Mon.-Sat. 8am-
midnight, Sun. noon-
9pm.
*This traditional 1950s style
Kaffeehaus is popular with both
younger and older locals, who
enjoy the vanilla and fruit tarts
while sitting in the velvet and pas-
tel surroundings. However, it's
quite expensive, so be prepared.*

Braunerhof
Stallburggasse, 2
☎ 512 38 93
U-Bahn Herrengasse
Open Mon.-Fri. 7.30am-
7.30pm
*Come here to read your newspa-
per in peace whilst eating a delicious warm Apfelstrudel. There's
an authentic Kaffeehaus feel to
the place, with its locals and its
waiters in tuxedos. At the weekend, you can enjoy live Viennese
music.*

Frauenhuber
Himmelpfortgasse, 6
☎ 512 43 23
U-Bahn Stephansplatz
Open Mon.-Fri. 8am-
11pm, Sat. 8am-4pm.
*This is one of Vienna's oldest
Kaffeehauser (1824) with a very
charming Biedermeier-style interior. It has a vaulted ceiling, wooden floors, deep red upholstery
and a good menu. Beethoven
was a frequent visitor here – why
not follow in the great man's
footsteps.*

Mozart
Albertinaplatz, 2
☎ 513 08 81
U-Bahn Stephansplatz
Open every day 8am-
11pm.
*Mozart is somewhat touristy, but
the service is friendly. If you didn't
manage to get a ticket to the
opera, you can console yourself
with a Mozart pancake for ATS75.*

Gerstner
Kärntnerstrasse, 11-15
☎ 512 49 63
U-Bahn Stephansplatz
☎ 512 49 63
Open Mon.-Sat.
10.30am-7pm, Sun.
10am-6pm.
*This famous Konditorei (pastry
shop) was founded in 1847.
Shoppers from Kärntnerstrasse
come to relax here and watch the
world go by. You can enjoy coffee, tea, a light lunch or even
Sunday brunch (11.30am-3pm).*

Oberlaaer Stadthaus
Neuer Markt, 16
☎ 513 29 36
U-Bahn Stephansplatz
Open Mon.-Wed. 8am-
7.30pm, Sat. 8am-6pm,
Sun. 10am-6pm.
*The prices here are excellent, and
it's a good place to buy Stollen,
those rich Teutonic Christmas
cakes full of fruit, nuts and
spices, direct from Oberlaa.*

Stubenviertel

**Eissalon
Schwedenplatz**
Franz-Josefs-Kai, 17
☎ 533 19 96
U-Bahn Schwedenplatz
*This Italian ice-cream parlour
just next to the station is famous
for its exquisite nocciolone.
However, its tiramisu ice cream
(ATS25) and tartufo, lemon
and vanilla flavours are worth
a try too.*

Karlsplatz/Naschmarkt

Museum
Friedrichstrasse, 6
☎ 586 52 02
U-Bahn Karlsplatz
Open every day 8am-
11pm.
*Adolf Loos designed this café in
1899, and Klimt and Kokoschka
were frequent visitors. It's chan-*

*ged a good deal since then, but
you can still come for a game of
billiards or chess while munching
on a tart or Strudel (ATS40).*

Schwarzenberg
Kärntner Ring, 17
☎ 512 73 93
U-Bahn Karlsplaz
Open every day 7am-
11pm.
*This is a classic Viennese
café with a marble and
wood-panelled interior and
huge mirrors. It opened in
1861 while the Ringstrasse
was still under construction.
There's live piano music
Tue.-Wed.8-10pm, Sat.-Sun.
4-10pm. Come here to read the
newspapers, including English-
language ones, or to buy one
of their many cigars.*

Imperial
Kärntner Ring, 16
☎ 501 10 356
U-Bahn Karlsplatz
Open every day 7am-
11pm.
*This is the place to come for
an Imperial Torte, a delicious
chocolate tart, or a blueberry
Strudel (ATS120).*

Drechsler
Linke Wienzeile, 22
☎ 587 85 80
U-Bahn Karlsplatz
Open Mon.-Sat. 3.30am-
8pm, Sun. 10am-
11.30pm.
*Early birds visit Drechsler for their
first coffee of the day while shoppers from the Naschmarkt
in need of a little refreshment
arrive later, and clubbers turn
up in the very late/early hours.
It's an atmospheric Kaffeehaus,
if a little scruffy.*

Alsergrund

Berg
Berggasse, 8
☎ 319 57 20
U-Bahn Schottentor
Open every day 10am-
1am.
*Berg is popular with gay and
straight locals, who all enjoy the
relaxed atmosphere, friendly service, tasty cakes and fresh fruit
salads. There's a bookshop next
door and it's a stone's throw from
the Freud Museum.*

Schottenring
Schottenring, 19
☎ 315 33 43
U-Bahn Schottentor
Open Mon.-Fr. 6.30am-
11pm, Sat.-Sun. 8am-
9pm.
Close to the Stock Exchange, this very elegant café is much frequented by brokers. There's live piano music, and in the evenings singers gather to perform opera songs. There's also a large selection of cakes.

Landstraße

Zartl
Rasumofskygasse, 7
☎ 712 55 60
U-Bahn Rochusgasse
Open Mon.-Fri. 8am-1pm,
Sat. 9am-6pm (closed
Aug.).
Zarti is known for its literary figures, past and prospective. Musil and Heimito von Doderer are among its famous clients. The decor is cream and green, and you can play billiards or just enjoy an ice-cream sundae.

Mariahilf/Neubau

Bortolotti
Mariahilfer Strasse, 22
U-Bahn
Babenbergerstrasse
☎ 526 19 09
This is the best Italian ice-cream parlour on Mariahilfer Strasse, with a wonderful selection of flavours.

Ritter
Mariahilferstrasse, 73
tel 587 82 38
U-Bahn Neubaugasse
Open every day 7.30am-
11pm.
If you're tired out after shopping, pop into this lovely oasis and enjoy a Strudel (ATS35).

Apollo
Windmuhlgasse, 32
☎ 581 65 33
U-Bahn Neubaugasse
Open Mon.-Fri. 7.30-2am,
Sat.-Sun. 2pm-2am.
This is a good place to come for a cup of tea or last coffee before going to the Apollo cinema located in the pink building opposite.

Wieden

Wortner
Wiedner Haupstrasse, 55
☎ 585 85 21
Tram 62 or 65
Open every day 9am-11pm.
This legendary variety café also has a restaurant, where the service can be slow. Turn up in the afternoon instead, and enjoy pancakes with nuts and whipped cream, or tuck into breakfast on a Sunday morning, with live piano music in the background.

Schönbrunn

Bawag
Am Platz, 6
☎ 877 93 38
U-Bahn Kietzing
After leaving Schönbrunn, pop into Bawag, where you can indulge in some low-calorie yoghurt or high-calorie delights, such as pear Strudel with whipped cream. You'll have the choice of the entire range of Viennese coffees (see p. 21).

Dommayer
Auhofstrasse, 2
☎ 877 54 65
U-Bahn Hietzing
Open every day 7am-
midnight (closed
Christmas Day).
The ballroom where Johann Strauss (the Younger) performed was to become the best café in the district. The waiters wear tuxedos and you can choose from a wide selection of coffees and cakes. It's a good place to come for refreshment after a day at Schonbrunn. Several romantic films have used the café as a setting.

CAFÉS

Cathedral

Sky-Box
Kärntnerstrasse, 19
☎ 513 17 12 25
U-Bahn Stephansplatz
Open every day 11.30am-4am.
This is an American bar on the seventh floor of the Steffl reached by a panoramic glass lift, from which you can gaze out over the rooftops of Vienna. The bar has wooden floors, and there's live piano music.

Loos Bar
Kärntnerstrasse, 10
☎ 512 32 83
U-Bahn Stephansplatz
Open Sun.-Thur. 6pm-2am, Fri.-Sat. 7pm-4am.
Adolf Loos designed this bar in 1908, the same year that his work on the pointlessness of ornament was published. Needless to say, there are few decorative features.

Dino's
Salzgries, 19
☎ 535 72 30
U-Bahn Stephansplatz
Open Mon.-Thu. 6pm-3am, Fri.-Sat. 6pm-4am.
This is an intimate and comfortable venue with excellent music and good prices. The house speciality is mango daiquiri, made of fresh mangoes, lime juice and Havana Club rum.

Onyx
Stephansplatz, 12
☎ 535 39 69 429
U-Bahn Stephansplatz
Open Mon.-Sat. 9am-2pm, Sun. 9am-6pm.
This café in the Haas-Haus turns into a bar at night, serving a few snacks at ATS120. The sofas are very trendy and the view of the Stephansdom Cathedral is wonderful.

Nightfly's
Dorotheergasse, 14
☎ 512 99 79
Open Mon.-Wed. 8am-3am, Thu.-Sat. 8pm-4pm, Sun. 8pm-2am.
Listen to Frank Sinatra and Dean Martin in an intimate club atmosphere, champagne cocktail in hand. This is the one place where you do need to dress smartly.

Stubenviertel

Castillo
Biberstrasse, 8
☎ 512 71 23
U-Bahn Stubentor
Open Mon.-Sat. 8pm-3am, Sun. 8pm-2am.
Try a 'Castillo Special', composed of rum, dry Martini, calvados, sherry and Angostura Bitters, served by some of the best barmen in town.

Duesenberg
Stubenring, 4
☎ 513 84 96
U-Bahn Stubentor
Open Tue.-Sat. 8pm-5am.
The bar isn't what it used to be, but the range of spirits and cocktails remains incredible. Give the house speciality, the 'Lisa', a try. It's a concoction of gin, lemon, pineapple, crème de cacao and melon liqueur. Delicious.

Karlsplatz

Maria Theresia
Kärntner Ring 16
☎ 501 10 39
U-Bahn Karlsplatz.
At Maria Theresia's there are three rooms, one circular bar and a largely lawyer-based clientèle sipping champagne or tomato juice. Claudia Schiffer look-alikes wait to be bought glasses of Canard Duchene.

Bristol
Mahlerstrasse, 2
U-Bahn Karlsplatz
☎ 515 16 0.
At Bristol you'll find photographs of famous personalities on the walls together with smartly-dressed waiters and subdued lighting. It's a peaceful, elegant bar, frequented by journalists and tourists.

Josefstadt

Edison
Alserstrasse. 9
☎ 409 55 99
U-Bahn Rathaus
Open every day 6pm-4am.
This relative newcomer to the list of cocktail bars has a good atmosphere despite its unprepossessing location. Try the 'Lawrence of Arabia' cocktail,

which is a mixture of rum, orange juice, mango syrup and coconut milk.

Rhiz
Lerchefenlder Gurtel, 37/38
☎ 409 25 05
U-Bahn Thaliastrasse.
Open every day 11am-4am (from 6pm Tue.)
This is a very unique bar for Vienna, a sort of Musikcafe and club all in one, with a DJ, jukebox, Internet facilities and drinks for ATS48.

Bermudadreieck

Ron con soda
Seitenstettengasse, 5
☎ 583 66 03
U-Bahn Schwedenplatz
Open every day 7pm-3am.
This buzzing West Indian bar serves delicious 'Long Island Iced Teas' and plays great samba music. The rum and daiquir cocktails are also worth trying. It's a popular spot with nightowls.

Der Neue Engel
Rabensteig, 5
☎ 535 41 05
U-Bahn Schwedenplatz
Open Sun.-Thu. 4pm-2am, Fri.-Sat. 5pm-4am.
The 'New Angel' was designed by the Coop Himmelbau, a deconstructionist group. It was formerly called the Roter Engel (Red Angel), though oddly its decor is black, gold and white. Music and videos are played in the background, and you can choose from Irish beer, Shiraz, fig liqueur and Haut-Adige wines.

Schottentor/Börse

Absolut
Borsegasse, 1
☎ 535 66 80
U-Bahn Schottentor
Open Mon.-Fri. 6pm-2am, Sat.-Sun. 8pm-2am.
If you're in the area, drop in and have a glass of the Swedish vodka, whose logo you'll see on absolutely everything that moves (or doesn't) in the establishment. Worth popping in if you're passing by.

Molly Darcy's
Teinfaltstrasse, 6
U-Bahn Schottentor
☎ 533 23 11
Open every day 11-2am.
This is an Irish pub which gets very busy in the evening. The staff are Irish, the beer is Irish and there are Irish books to read, should you get bored. It doesn't get much more Irish than this.

Spittelberg

Siebensternbrau
Siebensterngasse, 19
☎ 523 86 97
U-Bahn Volkstheater
Open Mon.-Sat. 11-1am,
Sun. 11am-midnight.
This is the place to come for some tasty and unusual beers. The Hanfbier made with hemp is worth a try.

Shamrock
Kirchengasse, 3
☎ 523 12 04
U-Bahn Neubaugasse
Open Mon.-Sat. 10am-2am, Sun. 5pm-2am.
This pub has an excellent selection of beers, but the food is less interesting. The atmosphere is warm and friendly, though.

Other districts

Myer's
Mayerhofgasse, 32
☎ 505 41 17
U-Bahn Taubstummengasse
Open Tue.-Sat. 6pm-3am.
This bar serves very potent brews, so beware. It's not for the fainthearted.

Karaoke Club
Buchengasse, 132
☎ 600 29 35
U-Bahn Matzleinsdorfer
Open Sat. from 8pm.
This bar is quite a distance from the centre but if you feel the urge to sing a Julio Iglesias song in front of a crowd of strangers, this is the place to come. It's in the 10th district and worth the journey for those three minutes of fame.

BARS & CLUBS

If you feel you've uncovered all Vienna's secrets and are looking for more adventures, there are two trips you can do by train quite easily. The first will take you to a small spa town that was the summer residence of the imperial court in the early 19th century. The second trip will transport you in a few minutes to the heart of a splendid Augustinian monastery, also known for its wine.

BADEN

It's very easy to get to Baden from Vienna. You can take the train or S-Bahn from the Südbahnhof in Vienna to the central railway station in Baden. It leaves every 30 minutes and is only a 20-minute journey, with a 10-minute walk to the town centre. Alternatively, take the Lokalbahn train, which leaves every 15 minutes from the station opposite the Staatsoper on the Ringstrasse. You'll reach the Josefsplatz just over an hour later. Whichever route you take, don't forget to put a swimsuit and towel in your bag, as there are forty thermal springs in Baden. A swim in the hot thermal baths is a real treat.

Before you dip your toes in, take a stroll round Josefsplatz and admire the Biedermeier façades. You won't be able to miss the stunning plague column in the Hauptplatz (main square). Take the pedestrianised Pfarrgasse to the Baden theatre, which is one of Austria's most beautiful theatres. It specialises in operettas, which are performed throughout the year. In winter, they're held at the Stadttheater, and in the summer they take place at the Sommerarena (summer arena). The ticket office at Theaterplatz, 7 is open Sun. 10am to noon, Tue.-Sat. 10am-1pm, 5-6.30pm. For more information call 02252 48 338 50.

From the theatre you can walk to the famous Kurpark, a lovely green space where the Viennese enjoy weekend strolls. This is the place to come for a picnic or pleasant walk. Alternatively, retrace your steps and head for Brusattiplatz, where you can buy fruit at the market stalls and try the tasty white wine from Gumpoldskirchen. At Brusattiplatz, 1 there's a wine cellar called the Badener Hauervinothek, which is open daily Apr.-Dec. 11am-7pm (10am Sat.), Jan.-Mar. Mon.-Fri. 2-7pm (10am Sat.). For more information, call 45 640. Just nearby there's an indoor thermal swimming pool (Mineralschwimmbad) that is open all year round. You're a hop and a skip away from Doblhoffpark, where you can relax in a mix of formal gardens and park, with an orangery, large rosarium, pond and pergola.

The thermal swimming-pool complex (Thermalstrandbad) is not far away on Helenenstrasse. You can swim in the open-air pools from May to September. The complex has a 1920s façade and was built in just 16 weeks. The water's wonderful, the temperature's perfect and a dip really is in order. If you're still feeling energetic afterwards, hire a bicycle at Voslauer Strasse, 38 ((492 22) or in front of the Südbahnhof in Conrad-von-Hotzendorf-Platz, 1 ((893 62 33). There are plenty of walking and cycle paths, so there's no excuse for laziness.

If you feel like staying the night in Baden, you could stay at the three-star Hotel Gutenbrunn at Pelzgasse, 22, (02252 48171. A double room costs from ATS700.

The Grand Hotel Sauerhof at Weilburgstrasee, 11-13, (412 510, is a little more chic and expensive (from ATS1600 for a double room).

KLOSTER-NEUBURG

Klosterneuburg is only 13km/8 miles from the centre of Vienna, and is one of the easiest day-trips from the city. Just hop on the

Wien-Tullin train from Heiligenstadt (U-Bahn U4), which leaves every two hours and takes only 10 minutes. You'll find yourself on the banks of the Danube at the foot of the stunning Augustinian monastery founded in 1114 by Duke Leopold III of Babenberg. The Spanish-bred Emperor Karl VI (1711-1740) wanted to build a huge imperial palace on the site, similar to the Escorial in Spain. Sadly it was never completed, but his ambitious plans are apparent in one wing. The greatest artists of the century worked on the building, and all the Baroque ingredients are in evidence – frescoes by Gran and Rottmayr, cascades of cherubs, spiralling clouds and pulpits glistening with gold.

The indisputed masterpiece of the monastery is the Verduner Altar, which was completed in 1181 by Nikolaus of Verdun and is in the Leopoldskapelle. It's made up of 51 gilded enamel plaques showing Biblical scenes, and is absolutely stunning. You can visit the monastery Monday to Saturday at 9am, 10am, 11am, 1.30pm, 2.30pm, 3.30pm and 4.30pm. On Sundays and public holidays, tours take place at 1am, 1.30pm, 2.30pm, 3.30pm and 4.30pm. The tour costs ATS50 and takes 45 minutes. For more information, (02243 62 10 212.

Your visit needn't end here – you can also pop along to the vast barrel-filled storeroom of one of the largest producers of Austrian wine, where you'll also find a restaurant. The Stiftskeller is on Albrechtsgasse, 1, and is open every day 1.30am-10.30pm for local wine tastings and food (☎ 02243 20 70). If you're in the vicinity on St Leopold's day in mid November, try and watch the barrel-rolling contest that takes place in the monastery.

If you have time, take a relaxing stroll along the winding Danube before catching the train back to Vienna. The last train leaves Klosterneuburg at 11pm, so there's no rush.

DAY-TRIPS

NOTES